P9-DEQ-783

THE Diamond Life

YOU ARE MORE THAN YOU HAVE BECOME!

TONY SCOTT

The Diamond Life Book
Published by Color House Graphics
3505 Eastern Avenue
Grand Rapids, MI 49508

ISBN 978-0-615-65474-4

Cover design by Highwire Creative
Cover photo by MarchCattle/Shutterstock.com

Dewey Decimal Classification: 269
Subject Heading: SPIRITUAL RENEWAL
Printed in the United States of America
January 2013 – First Edition

DEDICATION

To my wife, ShirleyAnn, my love, my life and best friend. Simply the most wonderful gem God gave to me. Your relationship with God inspires me, your support and encouragement motivate me and your love brings me joy. You make me better because you are a difference maker.

ACKNOWLEDGEMENTS

To Bill George, a true friend and colleague, who helped me frame the concept into a book.

To Lauren Clark, who spent countless hours helping me research and edit the manuscript.

To Tiffany Colter, Writing Career Coach, for your help through many resources.

To my loving family—Dave and Melony, Darin and Bronwyn, Olivia, Isabella, Mackenzie, and Abigail— you are the crown jewels in my life.

To my dear mother, Pauline, who taught me how to pray. To my extended family, Doris, Joyce, Don and Carol, you loved me even though I was far from home. Thank you for your support through the years.

To all those who came through the doors of the Church – to whom I've taught these principles over the years, you are some of the greatest and smartest Christians I know. You have enriched my life!

And most of all, to Jesus who chose me and placed me into His Kingdom.

CONTENTS

FOREWORD

The Diamond Life is a compelling disclosure and a clear reminder that God does not have the same perspective regarding people as we do. His perspective takes into account vistas we cannot comprehend.

Tony Scott is well positioned to write on the subject of God's transforming power. His own life is a brilliant example that it is possible to routinely and confidently walk in the goodness and power of Jesus our Master, accomplishing far more than human ability would suggest. One of the outstanding hallmarks of his ministry has been his influence in helping others reach way beyond what they thought they ever imagined they could.

In this book, Tony provides a strong mix of scriptural promises and practical help for putting our best dreams in motion. He focuses on the positive desires of the Christian life, which are so often neglected in Christian teaching. The incredible testimonies and insights shared in this book reveal that anyone can attain radiant living through the transforming power of Jesus Christ. It's time for each of us to expand our sights and embrace God's bigger picture for our lives. *The Diamond Life* is a powerful roadmap for this process.

—R. Lamar Vest, President/CEO American Bible Society

health that would require many surgeries over her lifetime.

Their story is important because it's indicative of The Diamond Life which I was privileged to watch them live. (I am happy to report I recently performed the wedding ceremony of their daughter who is living a happy, healthy Diamond Life.) Many years later, Sean was accused of fraud and learned he could face up to 20 years in prison. The pressure placed on his business, his marriage, his family, and his finances eventually brought him to the greatest challenge of his life. During this unexpected season of life, I watched him suffer through the devastating circumstances of the heat and pressure of these unjust charges. Not only did it take its toll on him mentally and physically, but the pressure was evident on his marriage, business, and finances.

My concern for Sean was how well he would hold up under the stress. If someone had told me he was going to go through something like this, I would never have believed he would handle it well. However, much to my surprise, he proved The Diamond Life formula really does work. His strength of resolve was never more evident than when he stepped up and allowed his faith in God to guide him through the most difficult challenges of his life. His extended family, his business colleagues and friends were amazed at how he withstood the stress and helped to lead all of them through this trying ordeal.

Thankfully, the issue was resolved and Sean and Lisa set about to reconstruct their lives. The heat, the pressure, and the time (more than 5 years of investigation) did not destroy Sean, his marriage, his family, and actually provided an opportunity for him to excel financially beyond his former business. Recently, he shared with me how the teachings through the years had caused him to be the man he is today.

As I looked into the face of Dylan and Leah (not their real names), the emotional pain was evident. It was a Sunday and that was to be their last day as husband and wife. The next day they were going to file for divorce. For some reason, I felt deep within me there was a better answer, a better solution to the traumatic series of events they were going through. Within minutes, we had set up a time of intervention and counseling which would help them navigate the rough waters that had resulted from some serious moral challenges. Dylan seemed eager and anxious to get started while Leah had that puzzled look that results when you mix deep emotional pain with a sense of hopelessness. What Dylan and Leah needed most was a redo, a makeover. They had not yet discovered the God-assigned potential of their relationship.

What happened in the intervening months and years is nothing short of a miracle. The heat, the pressure and the time–those powerful ingredients in creating a diamond–helped to recreate for Dylan and Leah, a beautiful marriage relationship. Together they learned how to weather the stormy season and discover the mystical union God intended for them. They refused to accept the ugliness that had crept into their marriage. And instead, they decided to find the diamond in the rough. Today, their marriage and family is a rich treasure of love, devotion and commitment. It is the picture of The Diamond Life formula.

What you are about to read is not just theory, it's been lived. Get ready for an incredible journey that has life-changing potential on every page. Regardless of where you are, regardless of your past, your sins, your failures, you too can live The Diamond Life.

"You" Discovered From Dirt to Diamond:

What You Don't Know About You

> **A diamond is a chunk of coal that is made good under pressure.**
>
> —HENRY KISSINGER

Ann Marie made the right choice. She decided at last that The Diamond Life was the only life for her, and she set out in pursuit of it.

For months before, the bright, animated college freshman with beautiful, flowing hair, an effervescent smile, and a bubbly personality had demonstrated daily such a faultless performance that no one in her world would have imagined the dark paths she had traveled.

As a vivacious, well-liked high school senior, Ann Marie had come under the influence of a friend who had manipulated her by duplicity and deception into a life of sensuality and lust that her closest friends could not have guessed. Her wake-up call came one day during her first year in college as she considered the person she was becoming, and with sudden clarity of thought decided, "This is not who I am and not who I want to be." Someone familiar with the Bible story of St. Paul's dramatic conversion might have called it Ann Marie's "Damascus Road" experience.

At that pivotal moment, she chose a path that began leading her toward a satisfying life that would be characterized by fulfillment and a robust spirituality. It's a life that I believe might best be labeled "The Diamond Life."

Really Good News!

What's this "Diamond Life" that was available to a young woman desirous of change and to anyone else weary and dissatisfied with where they are in life? I've brought you good news: there is such a life, and it is available to you!

For thousands of years, diamonds have been prized for their beauty, brilliance, and worth. The character of a diamond is marked by purity, clarity, hardness, and relative rarity. The Diamond Life is marked by similar distinctions. A man or woman arrives at The Diamond Life through a process comparable to the procedure that starts with a lump of carbon and ends with a scintillating jewel.

Mineralogists have revealed the circumstances that produce a diamond. It begins with a deposit of carbon in the depths of the earth—actually in its fiery mantle—that becomes exposed to almost immeasurable heat and incredible pressure for a lengthy period. The result of heat, pressure, and time is a gemstone that can reach staggering values, once it is freed from the deposit in which it is created.

Suppose I told you that before you were ever formed in your mother's womb a book had been written about your life. In the book, every day in your life was laid out—every plan, a destiny. In fact, every day in your life, you can discover that life—a Diamond Life. It is a process dealing with circumstance, trials, challenges, and difficulties; and through it you come face to face with who you really are: a diamond in the rough.

Certainly, in lucid moments of discernment, you may see yourself as an ugly lump of coal. Life seems without shape and seemingly without value. Forces have affected who and what you have become. Suddenly, however, the realization dawns that you do not have to remain who you are. There is more to life than what you have discovered. At that point, you can begin the process of realizing The Diamond Life.

It's Not Easy

I must caution you, however, that the process may require some unpleasant things: heat, pressure, and time. And today's culture wants to avoid heat, to escape pressure, and is impatient with waiting. Would you prefer that I tell you it's easy, effortless, and immediate? That's the message of self-styled gurus who offer an undemanding and painless journey to wholeness. Unfortunately, their results are fruitless.

Quite often you may be tempted to reject and even run from what has the power to reveal your true nature and identity. Everything about your creation speaks of three powerful truths contained within The Diamond Life: identity, purpose, and destiny. No human being arrived on Planet Earth because of an accident, a freak of nature, or a mistake. An incredible plan for life, direction for life, and equipment for the works of life was designed within you. And, in a time-release process as you interact with life, you come to discover who you are and why you are here. That journey, that process, is the most important part of your life.

Everyone was created to live The Diamond Life, but not everyone has chosen to do so. But, I think you can and should. Let's start by looking at the process.

CHAPTER ONE

"You" as a Diamond in the Rough

More Than You Think You Are

> **Many individuals have, like uncut diamonds, shining qualities beneath a rough exterior.**
>
> —JUVENAL

Have you ever thought about your life as a diamond, something polished, sparkling, bright, of great value? Or—to be totally honest—would you admit it has been ugly, pain-filled, conflict-ridden, remorseful, or regretful? I have tremendously good news for you—in spite of who or what you are today—concerning ancient, secret wisdom that can result in the total transformation of your life into all that you could ever imagine it to be.

You already recognize that the universe contains the secrets of beauty. All you have to do is look at the mountains, the oceans, the forests, the brooks and streams, and the rainforests to see incredible beauty not made by man's hands. The Hubble Telescope enables mankind to view majestic and glorious scenes of stars and galaxies, with brilliant colors beyond the most vivid imagination. Astonishing treasure is contained within the earth itself as miners excavate gems, precious metals, and, yes—diamonds.

Unseen Beauty

Hidden inside a lump of coal is found the most beautiful of all stones, created by three forces beyond the scope of man's ability to duplicate in their natural form: heat, pressure, and time.

Timeless wisdom from the past reveals a formula by which ugliness is transformed into beauty. The Diamond Life formula is not the product of man's ideas. Earth's natural resources produced the formula and continue to produce it. Man has discovered the formula and, with Divine help, has achieved the ability to apply it to the human life. Trapped inside of a lump of coal is the brilliance, the worth, the beauty of the diamond.

> A diamond in the rough is a diamond sure enough; For before it ever sparkled, it was made of diamond stuff. Someone had to find it, or it never would be found; Someone had to grind it, or it never would be ground. But once it's found and once it's ground And once it's burnished bright, That diamond's everlastingly just shining out its light.
>
> —ANONYMOUS

Diamonds were formed deep within the earth millions of years ago, crystallized from carbon into the world's hardest mineral. Recent experiments indicate that temperatures in the range of 5,000 degrees Fahrenheit must have been required, with pressure of more than a million pounds per square inch. This heat and pressure could have been possible only in the seething, boiling mass of molten rock in the mantle of the earth's crust.

The word "diamond" comes from the Greek word *adamas*, meaning "invincible" or "unconquerable." The phrase "diamond in the rough" pictures the opportunity for this undesirable-looking diamond to turn into something desirable and of great worth.

A diamond in the rough looks nothing like a diamond that has been cut, polished, and mounted. It's just an ugly rock. Your life, like a diamond, must be discovered, cut, polished, and mounted in its proper setting if it is to acquire the luster and brilliance God intended for it. Every phase of a diamond's production is uniquely important to the craftsman's plan to achieve a finished look. So is it also with you! Using the experiences of life, God takes every circumstance and every trial to shape you into the jewel He created you to be. Nothing is ever wasted.

Diamonds are highly-valued jewels, and a good quality diamond will often become a guarded investment. Diamonds begin their life after an extensive excavation process deep within the ground. A diamond must then go through what might be called the "diamond formula." To journey from a diamond in the rough to a highly-prized and sought-after piece of jewelry requires that it be discovered, crushed, cut, polished, and set into a distinctive place where it can shimmer.

Only a diamond can cut a diamond. Nothing can destroy, overcome, or change it, unless it's another diamond. The strength within the diamond protects it. It's your internal soul and spirit that makes you strong. That's the core, and that's where life transformation begins. You could be in the process of what I call a "shift." I'll say more about shifts shortly.

To separate the diamond from the piece of coal, roughly crushed and milled *kimberlite* is mixed with water. The light tailings rise to the top, and the concentrate falls to the bottom.

In one of several methods, an x-ray machine further separates the diamond from alluvial material. The diamond is cut and crafted for industrial use or jewelry.

In the "diamond life formula" God uses His Word to cleanse us and His Spirit to purify us of life's junk, garbage, and baggage.

He permits challenges in order to move us (a shift) from where we are to where He wants us to be. All the while He is increasing the value of our lives.

A shift is a very important part of your life. Look at

the technical definitions of a shift; there are several. First of all, *shift* means:

- ♦ to move or transfer from one place to another;
- ♦ to alter (position or place in life, an altering of where you are and what you are occupying);
- ♦ to change (gears, directions that you might be taking);
- ♦ to transition (move from one status, style or place to another).

Transitions can be good and they can be bad, but they come with life and are a part of life, moving from one status, one place, one style to another; a shift, altering, a change of directions.

All of these things make up the idea of a shift. Life is full of times of shifting. Wherever you are, and whoever you are: if there has not been a shift in your life, get ready for one, because it is coming. Seemingly, it always comes when you least expect it. Four words continue to affect us as we live on Planet Earth:

Transition

Change

Move

Shift

All four words will be part of your life as long as you are on this earth. You will go through moments of transition, change, move, and shift when you have to deal with the issues of your life.

Roger von Oech wrote that everyone has a "risk muscle." You must keep it in shape by trying new things. If you don't use the risk muscle it atrophies, it dries up, and it weakens. Make a point of using it at least once a day. Take a risk, take a chance, because when you risk something, new doors of opportunity open up. You go places you have not been before. You experience things you have never tried before.

Are you ready for some risk?

Separation

In your journey toward The Diamond Life, separation begins when you make a choice that you will no longer live the way you are living. At this point, you recognize your life is encumbered and burdened by junk, debris, and baggage that need to be separated from your life. Your goal is the discovery of the real you.

Every diamond is encumbered by black coal, dirt, and debris. There must be a separation in order to find it. One who searches for diamonds understands the need of a separation process.

Crushing/Cleansing

In the mining process, ore that is thought to contain

diamonds is passed through a crushing process, where pressure is applied to further separate the diamond-containing earth from alluvial material.

Often your life must go through a crushing process to clear away the debris that clutters your mind and clogs your spirit. The mind is renewed and the spirit is energized during this process. The hope of future beauty begins to take shape. In this step toward The Diamond Life, you move from the superficial to the more important depths within. You may not see immediate results; however, this inward process is absolutely necessary for your life to be properly molded and shaped.

As the diamond is washed and the small pieces of debris are crushed from it, it begins to reveal the hope of the beauty that was hidden inside. Now the diamond is ready to be cut and shaped.

Cutting

Buried deep within each person is an original purpose for living, a destiny. The molding process begins to shape a life to reflect the gifts, talents, and abilities hidden within. In this process, you can discover the "real you," not the person created by circumstances, trial, or pain, but The Diamond Life you were meant to live.

As a diamond is shaped, crafted, and cut to develop its various facets, so the facets of individual lives take on an outer beauty of an inward worth.

Mounting

Once the real you is set free—the "real you" who is living The Diamond Life—you are put on display and mounted for the world to be impressed and influenced by the beauty of your life.

The purpose of discovering the diamond is for it to be eventually mounted, so that others can see the beauty and value it contains.

All too often, an individual fails to become the person God created him or her to be. Buried beneath the excess weight produced by circumstance, conflict, and pain, there emerges a yearning for something better, something more. Like the diamond in the rough, your life needs to be washed, cleaned, shaped, crafted, cut, and mounted to become who you really are intended to be.

Even though you may not be prepared for it, even though you may not want to do it, a shift should never overwhelm you. Every time a shift is permitted into your life, it is for the purpose of lifting you to a better place. A God-shift is never intended to hinder, harm, or hurt you, but to make you better.

A shift may fix things for you. A shift may lift you. A shift is going to do a new thing in your life. Realize that sometimes new things will annoy you and make you uncomfortable. Coming out of your comfort zone will make you grow, though you may not feel great about it at the moment.

God is always working in and through you to perfect and sharpen you. Anything that God allows into your life will bring good. If it is in your life, just remember that He permits it for a reason. A God-shift always moves you into a new and better experience.

When you embrace a new thing, you must have a shift in your thinking. There must be a shift in the way you view life, the way you deal with life, the way you respond to life. When you shift, you must exercise the "risk muscle." A God-shift requires your complete trust in Him.

- ♦ A life-shift can move you from victim status to victor.
- ♦ A life-shift can change your disappointment into your purpose.
- ♦ A life-shift can move you from tragedy to triumph.

Look beyond your moment of distress and see the shift life is bringing. Stop hanging out in your past, remembering the "good old days." A shift will enable you to move from your "here" to your "there." You create your future from your future.

Are you ready for a better life than you have ever had before? Are you ready to move to a new level of living?

Maybe this shift will be to a new career. Although this new career interests you, it frightens you. Would you rather play it safe and work in a job that bores you? If you are losing interest in your job and don't understand why, perhaps a shift is taking place. If what you are doing doesn't interest you anymore, then a shift is taking place.

> **The more the diamond is cut, the brighter it sparkles; and in what seems hard dealing, there God has no end in view but to perfect His people.**
>
> —THOMAS GUTHRIE

As I thought about this shift, I remember the one that happened way back in a place called Eden:

It started in the garden with the very first man.
What happened to him was not in God's plan.
Instead of keeping his place, he decided to shift,
And from that moment on, his soul was adrift.
When you make a shift, a transition begins
And choices will determine where it all ends.
When God determines your life to shift,
He has in mind a positive lift.
Whatever the challenge, God will equip.
In the face of the task, you will never quit.
With every shift, there opens a door,
Opportunity beckons to make you soar.
Are you facing a shift in your life today?
By all means, you should stop and pray.
Hear exactly what God wants to say.

He will give you direction; then trust and obey.
Be strong in your hope and faith.
Shed every weight and finish the race.
A shift always means change and transition,
God is preparing you for a brand-new mission.

—Tony Scott

If God is ready to do a new thing in your life, the question for you is this: Will you embrace it? If so, then it's time for a shift into The Diamond Life.

Ann Marie wasn't necessarily ready to shift either. She couldn't see what her new life would look like. She had settled into the life she knew, the life she created for herself. But once she decided she was ready to make the leap of faith, she began to shift and enter The Diamond Life. Her life would never be the same again. She discovered she was more than she thought she was.

LIFE GEMS

From Chapter One

Inside of you is a diamond waiting to be discovered.

Life is full of times of shifting.

Remember to exercise your "risk muscle."

Buried deep within you is an original purpose for living, a destiny.

God is always working in and through you to perfect and sharpen you.

CHAPTER TWO

Redo "You"

Are You Ready for a Makeover?

You are one choice away from totally transforming your life.

Do you want to change your life?

Have you come to the point where you are saying, "I don't like how my life has been lived to this point, I want a new life, I want a redo"?

Ready For a Redo?

It really is possible. It's called *regeneration.*

Regeneration is a rebirth that produces a new life. It is part of the Diamond Life process. It brings excitement. It brings joy. Regeneration causes you to simply realize life other than the life you currently have. It starts with a reassessment of life. You look at yourself and declare, "I don't like the life I am living right now."

Good! You are now a candidate for regeneration.

God says, "You can start now and write a new ending to your story. I have placed someone within you whom you may not yet know. I put a person into you that you have not yet become. There is a 'real you' down inside of you who is not the 'you' created by circumstances. It's not the 'you' based on family. It's the 'real you' that I intended you to become before you were ever formed in your mother's womb. I made a decision about you and who I wanted you to be, and that person is in you waiting to be mined."

"*Re-*" is a prefix added to a word that causes it to mean "again" or "anew." You recognize it in words like "recreate" and "redo." It may carry the idea of going back and getting something right. English-speaking people like the concept of "*re-*" so much that the typical dictionary lists hundreds of word entries beginning with the prefix.

When generation is not enough, you need regeneration.

Generation is a chronological period of time in which a cycle in the succession of parents and children is produced; for example, grandfather, father, son—three distinct generations. The word *generation* and its derivatives also mean "to produce, to cause to be produced, to create." It's an action word, a production word, a creative word, a causative word, indicating making something happen. When you put the "re-"prefix with it, speaking of regeneration, you are talking about the initiation into a new state or a new form.

People have said to me, "I'm not happy with the

condition of my life." You can change the condition of your life. You don't have to keep living life as it is, you can change the form of your life. You can be regenerated. This word is powerful because it signifies "to do over or to make over into a better form."

Let me share with you a similar word—*reconstitute.* Reconstitute means to bring something back to its original state or to give new form to something: to alter the form of something. You can reconstitute your life. You can make your life over again. You can recreate it. You can have a makeover of your life if you are not happy with it.

Do you understand that there can be a Part Two or Part Three of your life? You can have something like a sequel to your life—a follow-up, a continuation, an extension, an expansion, and an increased life. A sequel is your opportunity, a time to get it right.

Charles Spurgeon, the best-known preacher of the nineteenth century, wrote: "Every generation needs a regeneration."

What Is Your LSQ?

To grasp what Spurgeon meant, I pose to you a question. What is your LSQ (Life Satisfaction Quotient)?

This is an extremely important concept, because you should periodically look at your life and ask yourself, "What meaning does my life have? What difference does it make that I am alive? How can I live a make-a-difference life?"

Let me challenge you to take the following LSQ survey:

- What is coming out of my life? What am I producing, creating, making or causing to happen?
- What comes out of me when life presses and crushes me?
- How important am I to God?
- How important is my daily living (quality of life) to God?
- Am I so important to the Kingdom of God that it's desirable for God to keep me alive?
- Who did God mean when He meant me?
- Who did He create when He created me?
- Did He create the person I have become by circumstance?
- Am I who I am because of someone else's decisions?
- Am I who I am because of my previous bad choices, my wrong choices?
- Am I who I am because of the culture around me, or because of what God says about me?
- What would I change in my life today if I could do so, without too much collateral damage?

- ♦ Where in my life would I like to push the redo button and retrace, fix it, and get it right?

The answers to those questions will reveal your Life Satisfaction Quotient.

When you know your LSQ, you will understand your need to transform your life. The definition of the word "transformation" can be broken down into three parts:

- ♦ "*Trans-*" means beyond, above, over.
- ♦ "*Form*" means the shape of substance, matter.
- ♦ "*-ation*" means action or result.

Transformation is the result or action of going beyond one's form. You are more, better, greater than you were before. It is your ability to think and go beyond your form that determines the quality of your life. Transformation takes you to the transcendent life.

What is the transcendent life?

- ♦ "*Trans-*" means beyond, above, over.
- ♦ "*-scendent*" means propelling forth, heaving.
- ♦ "*Transcendent*" means to exceed, to go beyond ordinary limits.

You should live a transformational life of transcendence. Changed people continually go beyond their "form" and continually exceed, or go beyond, current circumstance.

The process of becoming is what life is all about. In that process, you often struggle with certain hindrances, limits and opposing forces. You can be "transformed" but never "transcend." You must make that choice.

Each person is "wired" by God to live a real life of adventure that utilizes gifts, talents, and abilities to maximize fulfillment. You will never understand what you do not believe. Unless your faith takes you beyond your understanding, you will never grow.

Transformation is a process by which you become a fulfilled spiritual being. The following four steps will assist you in obtaining total transformation:

♦ **You were made to run life's race as a winner.**
People who desire to achieve success in life always give evidence of that. When you desire something with the whole of your being, you don't sit down passively waiting for it to come. If you want to live your best life, then you must declare it!

♦ **Discipline is one of life's greatest principles.**
Discipline has to do with activity, exercise, training, and education. Growth involves consciously eliminating from your life anything that does not assist in reaching your goal. It involves patiently building into your life the skills, habits, and actions that make your goal achievable.

♦ **Focus on your goal.**
Broken focus is one of life's greatest curses.

The discipline to focus enhances your ability to achieve results. No one would want to be operated on by a surgeon who is not focused. Focus sharpens your attention to detail and eliminates distraction.

- **Persevere through the challenge.**
  There is no increase of strength until you are striving against some force. This principle is seen vividly in any weight-lifting exercise. It is the resistance of the weights against the muscles that develop them. Your first opponent is always yourself. Without effort and struggle, no one can be a winner in life. All progress in whatever endeavor— material or spiritual—is due to opposition.

Transcendence helps you go beyond ordinary limits, beyond circumstances. Transparency causes the light (revelation) of God's presence to shine through you for others to see. You are transformed to transcend so you can become transparent.

God is asking you to look at your life and find the "real you" He created. There is nothing more important to your success than knowing the "real you"—the "real you" that's down deep inside at the core of your being. God created an identity for every individual on His Earth. No two people are alike. Just look at your thumb. Your thumbprint will match no other person's thumbprint. You are unique; He made you like no other. You were made with distinctive DNA. You were wired a certain way—your likes, dislikes, what turns you on and what turns you off. This is the "real you. " This is the "God-designed you."

If you want to live a long life, become important to the Father, and become meaningful to the Kingdom of God, produce something, make a difference. Don't just live. Don't just get up every day and go through the motions. That's not what life is about. You were born to produce.

What Is the Ultimate Result?

What will be the ultimate result of what you are creating 5, 10, 15, or 20 years down the road? What will be the ultimate result of the life you are living?

As you look at your life today—how much junk is there? How much stuff has been pressed down inside of you, buried deep in your spirit? How much junk is in your emotional makeup? How deeply embedded within you is the "real you"? How much are you willing to invest in the mining of the "real you"—the "you" God had in mind when He wrote the book about your life in Psalm 139?

> *For You did form my inward parts; You did knit me together in my mother's womb . . . My frame was not hidden from You when I was being formed in secret [and] intricately and curiously wrought [as if embroidered with various colors] in the depths of the earth [a region of darkness and mystery] (v. 13, 15, AMP).*

You and every person on the face of this green earth came with a book written about his or her life. You came hard-wired for your purpose. You have gifts, talents, and abilities. You have a purpose buried inside of you that came with you when God formed you in your mother's womb. Circumstance and people can't stop it. Even sin can't stop it. There is nothing that can be done by anything, or anyone to stop the purpose that God put in you. I want you to get the picture here.

I am talking about—

- ♦ The "real you", who along the road of life has been beaten up, tested and tried, traumatized and tangled, tempted and tainted. There are some things you have said or things you have done that the Enemy likes to remind you about.
- ♦ The "you" that the Holy Spirit is trying to activate into your fullest person, into your fullest destiny. That is the "real you" I am referring to—the one who is buried deep inside of you.

You can exist. You can be here; you can live and you can have a life. But if you want meaning, if you want purpose, if you want to reach your destiny, then you need to understand that your human form must be presented to God. Let Him fill your human life with Divine Life so that you may come alive and be the person He created you to be, and He will fill you up with His presence. In that moment, you are regenerated.

Regeneration cannot be hindered by your sins. What you've done and what sins you've committed can't obstruct you. Even if you've been married seven times and divorced, and the person you are living with now is not your partner, your husband, your wife, whatever. Even if you've had three, four abortions. It doesn't matter what the sins are. You can't sin your way out of the purpose you were born for. Jesus said, "I'll wipe your slate clean. I will cleanse you by My blood. I will restore and renew and make you the person that I've created you to be."

It Is a Divine Act

Regeneration is a divine promise, a divine benefit, and a divine work of God Himself. It has nothing to do with anyone but you and God. Nobody else gets involved in your regeneration. No one has any power over your regeneration, nobody can diminish it, hinder it, take it away from you, stop it. It's you and God.

In a manner of speaking, diamonds go through a "regeneration" process. They are hidden in alluvial ugliness, excavated from the ground, and then formed into something beautiful. Uncut diamonds need a redo, a rebirth, a regeneration.

Biblically, regeneration means to change, to renew, to remake, or recreate that which was generated.

It wasn't so long ago that we ourselves were stupid and stubborn, dupes of sin, ordered every which way by our glands, going around with a chip on our shoulder, hated and hating back. But when God, our kind and loving Savior God, stepped in, he saved us from all that. It was all his doing; we had nothing to do with it. He gave us a good bath, and we came out of it new people, washed inside and out by the Holy Spirit. (Titus 3:3-5, MSG).

There is available to you a change of state, a change of form and nature. God says, "I am going to make it possible for you to become brand new, to become someone that you haven't been, a change of nature—if you will—a change of form, a change of state. In the process of this regeneration, you are made free from the enslaving bondage of sin."

So if the Son liberates you (makes you free), then you are really and unquestionably free (John 8:36, AMP).

> **The soul is placed in the body like a rough diamond, and must be polished, or the luster of it will never appear.**
>
> **—DANIEL DEFOE**

Whoever you are at the core of your being will determine the substance of your life. Not who you are on the surface.

Not the face you wear every day. Not that artificial person, that pretend smile. I'm not talking about that. I am talking about the one at the depth, the core of your being. That's why people have trouble changing, because they change only at the surface. You can't change the surface and change anything. You have to go deep. You need to get to the core of your being.

I am asking you to join "the re-generation" and watch God perfect His purpose in your life. He will re-make, re-create, re-new, re-store you. You're going to love your makeover.

"Every generation needs a regeneration."

-CHARLES SPURGEON

LIFE GEMS

From Chapter Two

Your LSQ depends on your choices.

You will never understand what
you do not believe.

You become a winner as you discipline yourself
to focus and persevere.

You came hard-wired for your purpose.

Whoever you are at the core of your being will
determine the substance of your life.

"You" in 3D

From the Center to the
Surface and Beyond

You are spirit, you have a soul and you live in a body.

For You did form my inward parts; You did knit me together in my mother's womb. I will confess and praise You for You are fearful and wonderful and for the awful wonder of my birth! Wonderful are Your works, and that my inner self knows right well. My frame was not hidden from You when I was being formed in secret [and] intricately and curiously wrought [as if embroidered with various colors] in the depths of the earth [a region of darkness and mystery]. Your eyes saw my unformed substance, and in Your book all the days [of my life] were written before ever they took shape, when as yet there was none of them (Psalm 139:13-16, AMP).

The promise of the Creator is: Come to me and I will shape your life, make you its master, fill you with its fullness, uncover its hidden beauty, and energize you with its power.

Your heart is the switch to turn on His life inside of your being. Let him fill you up and run you over with His presence, with His power. Let Him get into every area, every facet of your life - mainly your spirit, soul, and your body.

Let Him come in. He will train you. He will teach you what your Diamond Life should look like. He will help you experience it. Don't obstruct the mining process. If you choose to be oppressed, you are obstructing the mining process. If you choose to be depressed, you are obstructing the mining process. If you don't have wisdom, if you don't have knowledge, you are obstructing the mining process. Get out of the way. He wants to reshape your life.

> **No pressure. No diamond.**
>
> —THOMAS CARLYLE

Diamonds, in their roughest form, endure the process of getting shaped before they are placed in a mounting. They are cut, clarified, color-designated, and weighed in carats. The maker takes the diamond and transforms it, shapes it, and makes it into something much different from its original state. This transformed diamond has value; it has worth. With the maker's skills and precision, it takes time, love, and careful chiseling to shape this diamond into its true form. Let Him shape your Diamond Life from the center to the surface and beyond.

CHAPTER THREE

Shaping "Your" Diamond Life

Measure the Treasure

> **The greatest treasure you will ever discover is that which the Creator put deep inside you.**

The Diamond's Clarity and Cut

- ♦ What would you attempt if you knew you could not fail?
- ♦ If in your life today there were no limits, no boundaries, no ceilings, no walls, nothing to restrict, and nothing to limit you from becoming whatever you feel you should become, what would you do?
- ♦ What would you attempt to do with your life if nothing was standing in your way?
- ♦ What would you need today to achieve the goals and the dreams of your life?

- ♦ What would you need to have to do it, to work it out?
- ♦ What are you currently exchanging your life for?
- ♦ What did you exchange yesterday for?
- ♦ In essence, what happened yesterday with your time? What did you do with it?

In order for your life to be re-shaped into The Diamond Life for which God created you, clarity and cutting—such as that performed on the diamond—must take place. The diamond must go through certain precise procedures in order to reveal its clarity and true shape.

Clarity

Clarity is a measure of internal defects, called inclusions, which could hinder the diamond's ability to transmit light. Though inclusions may degrade the value of the diamond because they are considered flaws, they are quite common. Inclusions, however, cannot be seen with the naked eye. Once the diamond is mounted in its setting, it is deemed virtually flawless.

Cut

The cut of a diamond describes the process by which the diamond has been shaped, polished, and formed into its final shape. The cutting of a diamond takes quality workmanship—long hours and precise craftsmanship. Every cut and touch of the chisel shapes the diamond and takes it one step closer to its mounting, its purpose.

The clarity and cut of a life are determined by the way a man or woman responds to life's circumstances. You always have a choice as to your response to what comes your way.

Rules of Life

Just as there are processes through which a diamond must pass to be perfected, life comes also with procedures and rules.

One of those rules says, "It's always darkest just before the dawn." (If you're going to steal your neighbor's newspaper, that's the best time to do it.)

Another rule of life says, "Before you criticize someone, you should walk a mile in their shoes." (That way, when you criticize them, you're a mile away and you have their shoes.)

Another rule says, "If at first you don't succeed, sky diving is not for you."

"If you lend someone $20 and never see that person again, it was probably worth it."

Recently, I ran across the Rules for Human Behavior. Here are the real rules for human behavior, and I think these are defensibly biblical.

Someone said:

Rule #1 You will learn lessons in life.

Rule #2 There are no mistakes, only lessons.

Rule #3 A lesson is repeated until it is learned.

Rule #4 If you don't learn the easy lessons, they only get harder.

Rule #5 You will know you have learned a lesson when your behavior changes; when you do something different from what you have been doing.

If those rules hold true for life—and I believe they do—then I think all of us will need some help.

> **You cannot control what happens to you, but you can control your attitude toward what happens to you, and in that, you will be mastering change rather than allowing it to master you.**
>
> —BRIAN TRACY

When God created man and woman, He always intended to be present in their lives. He wanted to guide, teach, and—yes—He wanted to coach for daily living. He shows how to do it and encourages that it be done right. He never intends for anyone to be a robot. He is always present to influence, encourage, teach, and show the right way to reshape life. He specifically sent His Holy Spirit to become a Spirit Life-Coach to direct 24/7 in the ways His followers should live. He wants each person to be positively influenced in every behavioral pattern, no matter what it entails. He wants the thought processes to be influenced—actions, deeds, words, decisions, choices.

There are three things extremely hard: steel, a diamond, and to know one's self.

—BENJAMIN FRANKLIN

The Imitation of Christ

Your behavior was intended by God to be a divine expression of His nature. He wants your daily activity, your speech, your communication, the way you share, and the way you live out your life to be an expression of His nature. To accomplish that, He placed in you a Divine Spirit within your human spirit. Your human spirit is the capacity He gave you to receive His life and to be re-shaped from the inside out.

Your Spirit Life-Coach

So what is a Spirit Life-Coach?

A Spirit Life-Coach is someone who will help you *clarify* your visions and goals. He will help you understand why you're on earth, what you are supposed to be living for. He will support you through your fears, keep you focused, confront your unconscious behaviors—your old patterns, your old self, your old way of doing things.

Using the diamond formation vocabulary, in the *cutting* process, He constantly helps you confront the old behaviors and old patterns in your life. But He doesn't stop there. He says "I want to influence you to make the best choices, the best decisions. I want you to hear My voice speaking inside of you. I want to help you live by Spirit-motivated values. I want to keep you focused on the core giftings of your life. I want you always operating out of who you were created to be and what you were created to do." In the process of clarifying and cutting your life, hindrances are removed to better shape you for your display. This is always the work of the Holy Spirit Life-Coach.

The Bible teaches why the Holy Spirit came:

> *I will ask the Father and He will give you another comforter: A counselor, a helper, an intercessor, an advocate, a strengthener, a stand-by. I am going to give you the Holy Spirit and He is going to come and the world won't see Him, the world won't recognize Him, but you will see Him, you will recognize His works. You will see that He is influencing you on a day-by-day basis to do the right things (John 14:16-17, AMP).*

He is going to remain with you forever. He is not going to leave you; He is not going to forsake you. He is going to be there. He is the spirit of truth.

> *The Counselor, the Holy Spirit,*
> *Whom the Father will send in My name*
> *(John 14:26, AMP).*

He will be a teacher. He will teach you all things—everything going on in your life. Not only will He teach you all things; He will cause you to recall, to remember things you have learned, thought of, done; things you want to do, that you ought to think about. He will help your memory. In this process of clarity and cutting, God is adding value to your life.

A diamond with a flaw is worth more than a pebble without one.

—CHINESE PROVERB

Furthermore, the purpose of a Life-Coach is to empower you to be better than you are, to do more than you are doing, and to do it in a better fashion. A coach is needed because you don't know what to do or how to do it. His promise is of growth and development. "I will grow you. I will develop you. I will increase your value." A good coach will help you be a better "you." He will increase your value.

A Life-Coach is in charge. He helps you in what you are attempting to do, and turns up the pressure, so you can do it better. The Holy Spirit has been on the scene from the beginning. Without the Holy Spirit, there would have been no creation of the world. Without the Holy Spirit, there would have been no creation of man. The Spirit of God did these things. He was active in the beginning, and never intended not to be active. He always wants to be in charge of your life. He never wants to be relegated to a secondary position. He wants to be your Life Coach every day of your life.

As a Spirit Life-Coach, He teaches, advises, corrects, instructs, trains, tutors, guides, directs, and prepares you for whatever life brings. He shows you what you need in your life.

What is the Holy Spirit doing when He permits challenges in your life? He is trying to teach you about you. He is not trying to learn about you; He has known you since before you were born! He is saying to you…

He miraculously brings you into His plan. His presence empowers you to walk out your faith. He opens up God's Word to your spirit and your mind so you can think the very thoughts of God and actually live the ways of God. He helps you to think properly.

Everything that is in your life, He allowed, and it comes by His will. He can stop anything from coming into your life at any time. What He permits has a purpose, but that doesn't mean you understand it or you like it. If a diamond could speak, it would certainly be complaining during the process it's being put through. In the same manner, God designs circumstances to benefit your life. Since He knows you better than you know yourself, He properly proportions the adversities that are necessary to perfect (clarify and cut) and shape your life.

You are bigger than you think you are.
You are more beautiful than you think you are.
You are more brilliant than you think you are.
You are more than you think you are.
You are unique.

Going Deep

The greatest journey you will ever attempt and travel in your life is the one that takes you deep inside your spirit to discover the things of God.

Inside each of us, there is a database from which we get the answers about our life. Just as there is a diamond in a lump of coal, there is a Diamond Life inside of you, waiting to be re-shaped by an ever-present God. Often, people go around in circles searching for wisdom and knowledge for the complexities of life. Sometimes they are told they need a good counselor, intellectual, psychologist, or psychiatrist to help fix what seems to be wrong. All the while, they have within the answer—the releasing, the shaping, and the mounting of The Diamond Life.

Occasionally, God will let finances become challenging, just to seize attention. Sometimes, He will permit tests that will result in new wisdom and knowledge. Life occasionally brings attacks for which no preparation has been made. God allows these challenges. He's in the process of perfecting you. This is the diamond formula; He's shaping the diamond you are intended to be. He's putting you through heat, pressure, and an extent of time, so He may work through you.

The Spirit Life-Coach, who is the Holy Spirit, is looking for a setting, a place that affords seclusion and separation from the pressures, anxieties, and responsibilities of life. He is looking for an opportunity to teach you something you don't know. He wants to reveal you to you.

The Spirit Life-Coach can't teach people whose minds are constantly cluttered. How can you organize your mind when you look at things on your desk and they are prompting a thousand thoughts? How do you order your mind when you look at your calendar or your agenda and there is so much to do? How do you arrange your mind when each day you wake up, all your waking hours are filled with e-mails, phone calls, Facebook messages, tweets, texts, LinkedIn alerts, and so forth? God is always saying, "Where's My place, where's My time, when will you block off a moment for Me and let it just be you and Me?" When will you come to the place that you let the Holy Spirit begin to instruct you and guide you so your mind is solely on Him? It is in moments like these that He can be shaping your Diamond Life.

As the jeweler crafts the diamond, he becomes intimately engaged with every facet of the process. He is creating a thing of beauty, something to be desired, something of true worth and value. No craftsman would attempt to casually cut a diamond. He becomes intimately involved with the process, so much so that it might be said he develops a love affair with it.

This requires a level of intimacy beyond the casual or flippant. Analyze that word with me: *intimacy*. Pronounce it this way: *in-to-me-see*. When you permit the Holy Spirit into the deepest level of your life, then you have intimacy with Him. It is not as though you can hide anything from Him anyway. Invite Him to a level of trust, friendship, dependence, and love beyond anything you have experienced.

The diamond cutter takes great pride in bringing the diamond to its exact form and most perfect shape that is required for its mounting and display. There is no place for shallowness. He intricately, delicately, cautiously dedicates his ability to shape the diamond for its greatest value and worth. Only when he sees the diamond in its final form does he feel the sense of pride and joy that went into the shaping.

That is exactly the way God feels about you. Beyond the superficial, the shallow, He desires the deepest level of intimacy, which allows access to the innermost being. It is there a love affair develops that brings out the best in you. It's personal—just between you and God. You know and experience Him on a level you've never known before. He then can use and display your life for your greatest good and His greatest glory. This shaping of The Diamond Life is made possible only if you permit the hand of God to precisely, tenderly touch the strings of your heart and bring to a fantastic display the diamond inside of you.

If you only look at us, you might well miss the brightness. We carry this precious Message around in the unadorned clay pots of our ordinary lives. That's to prevent anyone from confusing God's incomparable power with us. As it is, there's not much chance of that. You know for yourselves that we're not much to look at. We've been surrounded and battered by troubles, but we're not demoralized; we're not sure what to do, but we know that God knows what to do; we've been spiritually terrorized, but God hasn't left our side; we've been thrown down, but we haven't broken. . . . So we're not giving up. How could we! Even though on the outside it often looks like things are falling apart on us, on the inside, where God is making new life, not a day goes by without his unfolding grace. These hard times are small potatoes compared to the coming good times, the lavish celebration prepared for us. There's far more here than meets the eye. The things we see now are here today, gone tomorrow. But the things we can't see now will last forever (2 Corinthians 4:7-9, 16-18, MSG).

The Treasure of the Lord

You become, in your weak frail body, the dwelling place of the Holy Spirit and inside you is the treasure of the Lord. You are God's greatest treasure. You are worth more to Him than a star, the sun, the earth, the moon, and all of them put together. You are worth more than the planets. There is nothing on any planet worth as much as you. He didn't die for a planet, He didn't die for a star, He didn't die for the sun, He didn't die for the moon—He died for you. He gave His life for you. He says, "You are my treasure. You are so important to me; you are so valuable to me. I've invested everything I have in you." The richness and the fullness of the Kingdom of God are yours. You are flooded with God Himself, with His wisdom, His knowledge.

So, why does anyone continually foul up? Why do they get it wrong? It's because mankind is driven by the desires of the body rather than the desires of the spirit. Men and women are God's investment, His treasure.

The treasure of God is inside you, and He is making it even more available to you according to the maturity of your faith. The more you trust, the more you believe, the more He allows you to enjoy the blessings and the goodness of His Kingdom. He is constantly saying to you, "You are my investment. That's why I am continually clarifying and cutting you into your Diamond Life."

> **He who finds diamonds must grapple in mud and mire, because diamonds are not found in polished stones. They are made.**
>
> **—ANONYMOUS**

The Holy Spirit is fitting you, building you, shaping you, and making you into a habitation of God. And the better, the more beautiful, the more powerful the habitation of God you are, the more beautiful, the more valuable, the more glorious your life will be. Your life shines with the beauty of who God is and what God wants to do within you and through you.

Has your life become more beautiful and valuable because of what God has done in you and through you by the power of the Holy Spirit? God's standard of measurement for your life is the development of His purpose through you, thus determining the measure of your treasure.

LIFE GEMS

From Chapter Three

You have available to you a
Spirit-Life Coach.

Your Spirit-Life Coach will empower
you to be better than you are.

You are more than you have become.

You are God's greatest treasure.

Only God can determine the measure
of your treasure.

CHAPTER FOUR

Wholly "You"

Weight for Your Worth

> **Guard well your spare moments. They are like uncut diamonds. Discard them and their value will never be known. Improve them and they will become the brightest gems in a useful life.**
>
> **– RALPH WALDO EMERSON**

Remember Ann Marie, the young woman you met early in the book? She came to a dramatic moment when she said, "This is not who I am. This is not who I want to be." That decision was made by her, but it was prompted by the Holy Spirit, who always desires the best for each of God's creations.

Into created life, God puts His uncreated life. His purpose is to empower and enable men and women with given tools to live in victory and peace on a day-by-day basis. He never intended mankind to be overwhelmed by the challenges of daily lives. He never intended for life to be burdened with unnecessary baggage.

No one can live a fruitful, fulfilled, significant life

without having a renewed mind. He promises to give you a new heart, a new spirit, but you will need to renew your mind. The renewing of your mind becomes your responsibility since you have to make a choice about God. Remember, He chose you before you were in your mother's womb. Now you must choose Him. No one can live a fulfilled life, no one can live a significant life, and no one can live a self-actuated life until they come to the place of having a renewed mind. The renewing of the mind must be done on a continual basis.

A new heart will I give you and a new spirit will I put within you, and I will take away the stony heart out of your flesh and give you a heart of flesh (Ezekiel 36:26, AMP).

How powerful is the mind! It can believe rightly and secure a place for you in heaven. Whatever you hold in your mind, whatever is your strongest and most dominant thought, what you dwell on the most will normally, naturally, over time, begin to occur in your life.

The mind is its own place, and in itself can make a heaven of hell, or a hell of heaven.

—JOHN MILTON

If you continue to believe as you have always believed, you will continue to act as you have always acted. If you continue to act as you have always acted, you will continue to get what you have always gotten. The only way that your life is going to change is by your experiencing a change of mind.

Finding the Diamond's Carat and Color Carat

The *carat* measures the weight or mass of a diamond. A diamond that carries more carat weight has more worth. However, the cutting and polishing of a diamond often results in a dramatic loss of carat weight, up to 50%, because there is so much dirt and debris around the true beauty. Because the cutters are trying to avoid too many inclusions and flaws in the diamond, they are willing to compromise the weight of the diamond to bring it more overall worth.

Just so, God will often eliminate from your life things you think are important, but in His divine judgment are unnecessary.

- ♦ Who is adding to your carat value?
- ♦ Do you have extra baggage in your life?
- ♦ Who or what compromises your carat value?
- ♦ Who or what devalues you?

Color

Diamonds are graded with a color system that adds to the value of the diamond. Diamonds near the grade of colorlessness are highly valued; however, most diamonds found in jewelry stores have slight hints of yellow or brown. Although it may be almost invisible to the eye, color will affect the cost of the diamond. However, when diamonds are placed into their settings, any small amount of color that they hold is not obvious, nor is it possible to make out color shades. Because the diamond is on the mounting and the light is able to pass more easily, the color seems to disappear.

Often your life may be colored by things you permit, but you know they can bring harm in some way. Who or what are you allowing to affect your life? Precious, valuable diamonds are colorless, pure. They are the best they can be. You need your heart to be colorless, sinless, pure, and free from blemishes. Are you ready for that pure heart?

Sometime individuals forget they are more than physical human beings. Each person is made up of three distinct and separate parts:

Spirit | Soul | Body

God is always trying to remove anything in the spirit, soul, and body that lessens the value of your life.

- The *spirit* is your God-consciousness. It is the part of you where He makes you aware of Him. God teaches you about Himself. It is from the spirit to the heart, to the mind, to the body that you live. At least, that is the way that God intended for you to live.

- The *soul* is your self-consciousness—that is, your mind, will, emotions, and desires.

- The third part is your *body*, which is your sense-consciousness. Five senses guide your life on a day-by-day basis—seeing, hearing, tasting, touching, and smelling.

It is important to understand that, in spiritual language, the heart (not the physical organ) is the term used to designate the seat of your emotions. Out of it comes all communications—good and bad, positive images, bad images, positive messages, bad messages. Your heart needs to be filled with His presence. Your heart is the location of your personality. Where your heart is, you are. What your heart is, you are. Your heart determines the course of your life.

God looks on the heart. From your spirit, He speaks to your heart.

This conquering principle of life is an inward renewal that brings about transformation in our lives.

**God speaks to your heart –
your heart speaks through your mind –
your body responds to your thoughts.**

A Brilliant Life

The brilliance of a person's life is never from outside to inside, but from the inside to the outside. That brilliance comes only by the process of His wisdom and knowledge coming through your spirit to your mind until your bodily actions shine with His glory. This is life from the inside to the outside.

An example of this is seen in Mark 9 when Jesus tells his disciples of the coming Kingdom of God.

> *Six days later, three of them did see it. Jesus took Peter, James, and John and led them up a high mountain. His appearance changed from the inside out, right before their eyes. His clothes shimmered, glistening white, whiter than any bleach could make them. Elijah, along with Moses, came into view, in deep conversation with Jesus (Mark 9:2-4, MSG).*

Suddenly Jesus became brilliantly white. He was glowing. This glory they saw came up out of His inner being and was made transparent. They saw His inward nature. They saw the beauty and the glory of who Jesus was on the inside.

Have you ever said about someone, "She is as beautiful inside as she is outside"?

Jesus said, "You are the light of the world. I want the brilliance of My light to come up out of your inner being so the world can get a picture of Who I am in you. I want the world to see Me in you. I want you to have My light on your face. I want you to get a bright smile on your face. I want you to be excited, energetic, pumped, powerful people out in the world revealing the glory of Me."

Diamonds sparkle and shine more brightly when they are in the light.

A Renewal of Life

The word *renewal* means "a complete renovation of thought."

Jesus says, "I want to renovate your thought life. Man possesses free will, and because of that, God provides His word and His spirit to renew your mind so you can discipline and control your thoughts and imagination."

You get a heart transplant from God, a regenerated spirit and then the Master Physician provides "brain surgery" on your mind. God is working 24 hours a day, seven days a week in you. You are never alone. It may be that you feel alone, isolated. Sometimes you may feel as if no one else is suffering or going through what you are experiencing. But everyone suffers these kinds of attacks. When this happens, you can run to God and fill yourself with His Word. His Word comes into your spirit, through your heart, into your mind, and your life begins to line up with the revelation of God.

Either that which is outside of you—circumstance, environment, culture—or that which is on the inside of you will determine how you think and act.

You can have the peace of God. You can have a new heart. You can have a new spirit. You can have a constant renewing of your mind by the Word and the Spirit. The greatest day in your life is the day you decide that your life is not your own—it belongs to Jesus Christ. You are not your own, but you are bought with a price. Jesus becomes the power of God within you and He becomes responsible for every surrendered life that is lived in two dimensions—discipline and dependence. God gives you those two powerful words to live by.

I am His diamond.
He purchased me.

He wants you to live by His "red letter" words—those teachings that came directly from His lips—and they become the rules by which you govern your life. He also wants you to live by discipline and depend upon Him.

No one ever conquers life unless that person first conquers self. No one ever lives a better life for himself or herself until that person creates a better self. If you want to live a better life, you must become a better person. It starts with you; it starts within your mind.

Concerning your mind, the Bible lays out only two choices: Either you will rule your mind, or your mind will rule you. You will dominate it or it will dominate you. You will discipline it or it will control you.

You cannot stop thoughts from entering your mind; however, you can control what you do with those thoughts. Discipline is not about stopping a thought from coming in; discipline has to do with your response to it.

- ♦ Do you kick it out?
- ♦ Do you cast it aside?
- ♦ Do you put it down?
- ♦ Do you crush it?
- ♦ What do you do with the thought once it hits your mind?

God's Word is knowledge. Knowledge helps us to gain wisdom and understanding. Once you obtain knowledge, you must understand the knowledge. If you understand the knowledge, you will operate in wisdom. That's how God's process works: knowledge leads to understanding and understanding results in wisdom.

For God did not give us a spirit of timidity (of cowardice, of craven and cringing and fawning fear), but [He has given us a spirit] of power and of love and of calm and well-balanced mind and discipline and self-control (2 Timothy 1:7, AMP).

God says, "If you want to live the best life, if you want to live the most powerful life, if you want to live the overcoming life, if you want to live fulfilled in this life, then you take what I've given you—not a spirit of fear, but of power, love and a disciplined mind."

The word *fear* is "timidity" and it has a number of meanings. It means weakness, embarrassment, shame, frailty, fearfulness, and cowardice. And God is saying to you, "I have not given to you a spirit of fear. I don't want you to be weak. I don't want you to be frail. I don't want you to be embarrassed. I've given you gifts. I've enabled you with Holy Spirit gifts to stand up in the world and live a righteous life and not be ashamed of the gospel of Jesus Christ. I've given you a spirit of power. You will be forceful, powerful in your daily living."

God wants you to have a sound or disciplined mind. He says, in essence, "If you believe My Word and My Word comes up into your mind, there will be a renewal of your mind according to discipline. You won't be fearful, you won't be timid, you won't be shy, you won't be frail, you won't be weak in the midst of the opposition. You will be able to stand up with a disciplined mind, without fear, and take on life and you won't be oppressed, depressed, or overwhelmed, because I've given you the power of a sound or a disciplined mind."

Sound or *disciplined* mind means the control of one's self in the face of praise or pain. It is ultimate self-control.

Self-discipline begins when you wake up to the fact you are living with undisciplined thoughts in your mind that must be conquered. The whole world of achievement which is around you belongs to the person who will simply do one thing: exert the willpower to discipline the thought life. Just start thinking like God wants you to think and give into the presence of His Spirit.

Your thoughts shape your behavior—more than facts, more than circumstances, more than people, more than the economy. What you think determines the quality of your life.

When people are close to one another, they affect each other. It's a fact of life: you take on the nature of the people with whom you spend the most time. We grow similar to those whom we live with. Let only the Holy Spirit shape you, and let others sharpen you.

The Holy Spirit is a filter through which your thoughts can pass. He evaluates everything that enters, and He says to you, "This is good, this is not so good. This is a ten, this is a five." He nudges you to make the right choices; He filters out the junk, and lets you know what is the good, the acceptable, and the perfect will of God. However, the direction of your life is determined by your choices.

Ella Wheeler Wilcox sat by the East River in New York watching sailing vessels coming up the river. She was thinking about children and their families. One child was near perfection and another child was as disobedient as can be. She was wondering why there could be such differences among members of the same family with the same mother, same father, same siblings, and the same atmosphere. And as she thought about it, she wrote these words:

> **One ship drives East and another drives West,**
> **With the selfsame winds that blow.**
> **'Tis the set of the sails and not the gales**
> **Which tells us the way to go.**

- ♦ Which wind is blowing on your sails?
- ♦ Which winds are directing the course of your life?
- ♦ Is it the wind of circumstance?
- ♦ Is it the wind of family heritage?
- ♦ Is it the wind of family tradition?
- ♦ Is it the wind of family faults?
- ♦ Is it the wind of habits?

You can choose to be driven by the wind of His Spirit and the wind of His Word.

Whatever is true, whatever is worthy of reverence and is honorable and seemly, whatever is just, whatever is pure, whatever is lovely and lovable, whatever is kind and winsome, and gracious, if there is any virtue and excellence, if there is anything worthy of praise, fix your minds on them (Philippians 4:8, MSG).

He helps you sift through the dirt. He holds you and comforts you as you are sifted through the shaking process. But as you are sifted, you're letting go of junk, you're letting go of your past. You're entering into the diamond process. Once the process is complete, you will see your value. You will see the wait was worth it.

LIFE GEMS

From Chapter Four

Into your created life, God puts His uncreated life (eternal).

To change your life, you must change your mind.

Your heart determines the course of your life.

The greatest day in your life is when you decide it belongs to Jesus.

You cannot conquer life until you conquer yourself.

What you think determines the quality of your life.

"Your" Diamond Setting

Revealing Your Light, Fire, Brilliance

**Wherever you find yourself,
His intention is for you
to shine and radiate His life.**

After the refining of the diamond (cut, clarity) it is then ready to be set or mounted. This involves rising to a higher point, or ascension. God is always delighted when He can lift us to a place where we have not been and showcase His life though us. That's how we become a *light* to the world.

The term *light performance* is used to describe how well a polished diamond will return light to the viewer. There are three light properties described in relation to a diamond's light performance: *brilliance*, *fire*, and *scintillation*.

Diamond *brilliance* is defined as the reflection of light from the diamond's facets. The more the diamonds have been cut and polished by the gem cutter, the greater amount of reflection will be produced.

Diamond *fire* refers to the spectral colors produced as a result of the diamond dispersing the white light.

Scintillation describes the small flashes of light that are seen shooting from the diamond, when the diamond's light source or the viewer moves.

A diamond cut and polished to produce a high level of these qualities is said to be high in *light performance*. It is the light of the real you that brings attention to your true value.

CHAPTER FIVE

The Real "You" on Display

Location, Location, Location

> **No diamond is mined to be placed in a drawer or case. It is mined to be mounted or set.**

Once the diamond has been shaped through cutting, clarified, weighed in carats, and assigned a color, the diamond is ready to be put on display.

- ♦ How does God want to use me to make a difference in the world?
- ♦ What does He want to do with me?
- ♦ What is He expecting from me?
- ♦ What is He looking to get out my life as I live in the here and now?
- ♦ How do I get to where He wants me to be?

The answer: Use the Global Positioning System (GPS). When you want to know how to get to "there" from "here," it's the gadget of choice. In order to understand directions, you must know two things: where you are and where you want to go. Those two things are critical if GPS is going to work for you.

All of the GPS devices work on the principle of a "here" and a "there." You punch in the "here" and you punch in the "there," and then you get the direction.

OnStar®, a commercial GPS application, depends on a computer chip in a vehicle that communicates with a satellite in space. A GPS device, using the OnStar® chip, can locate your car by using the satellite, and call emergency responders if you need them. If you have OnStar®, you can never really get lost, because it enables an eye in the sky.

The God Chip

In Genesis 2, when God made Adam and Eve, he put a "God chip" inside of them, and the "God chip" was passed on to every person. In a sense, there is a piece of God in every individual or we couldn't be alive, because life only comes from God. You and I are made by God with a "God chip"—a piece of Himself—which always tells God your "here." Every part of man was a part of the earth except the blood. God made the blood. The life of God is in the blood; that's where you receive the God-chip.

If you know where you have been and where you are going, you never have to worry about where you are. You do have to know where you are, but you never have to worry about where you are, if you are serving God.

You will never arrive at your "there" if you don't live in your "here." You must fully comprehend the "now" moment in order to get to the place where God wants you to be. Here is what God did: He designed a unique "there" for every single person on the face of the earth. And for each person, the journey to "there" is equally unique.

"There," as a definition, is where you face the issues of life. God designed you to experience a full and complete life. "There" is a place where you will know, where you will experience, and where you will fully comprehend the life God created for you. All the things about you make you unique. Your likes, your dislikes, the things you love, the things you hate, the things that turn you on, and those that turn you off. Everything about you that makes you unique was designed for a "there" where God wants to take you and He designed for you to experience.

Ask yourself some questions:

- Did you choose this physical, geographical location to be living your life in, at, on, today?
- Is your "here" a place you have chosen?
- Is your "here" a place someone or something has chosen for you, a place that your hurt, pain, disappointment, circumstance has chosen?
- Is your "here" a place of disappointment?

- Is your "here" a place of pain, is it a place of anger?
- Is it the "here" you have chosen, or it the "here" God has chosen for you—your purpose and divine destiny?

Before you answer those questions, let me advise you that your "here" may of necessity be a place of great comfort or of great discomfort. It might be a place of great conflict or it might be a place of peace. When God chooses a place for you, He has ulterior motives for you to be there. Always in your "here," God has something He is saying to you.

Until you become obedient to His will for your life, you cannot move from your "here" to your divinely designed "there." It is impossible for that happen. You can make all of the arguments you want to make, but you better come to a moment in your "here" when you find favor in the sight of God, when you allow God to show you what His favor is.

A Place of Favor

To *favor* means, "to give special regard to, to treat with exceptional kindness, to give preferential treatment."

In the Bible, *favor* means "grace, pleasure, acceptance." God is saying, "Here is my favor. Here is my grace. Here is a pleasant moment for you in your 'here.' I affirm you. I accept you."

Not only will God favor you, but He will distinguish you. *Distinguished* means "marked out, distinct, unique, special."

There is a word in the Old Testament for *anointing* which means "target." You have been "targeted" for a blessing. You are looking at your "here" and asking, "Where is the blessing? There is no favor here. I don't want to be here." But God says, "You are the anointed of the Lord, I've painted a target on you; if you will stop complaining, I will show you something good where you are that will distinguish you from anyone else who's where you are."

Occupy your "here." God is waiting for you to listen. He wants you to get to your "there." Where is your "there"? It's on that special setting, that mounting. God wants to place his diamond upon the mount for the world to see. He wants to show you off. He wants to be involved in your victory and celebrate with you. You were meant to get "there."

"For you were bought at a price; therefore glorify God in your body and in your spirit, which are God's"
(I Corinthians 6:20)

Since you were bought with a great price, honor God and glorify Him in your body.

The word *bought* is the word "to redeem" or redemption. You are redeemed with a price. The word *redemption* actually means "to locate." When God redeemed you, He located you. He came to your "here" to find you. He came to redeem your moment. He came to take you from your moment and to put you in your "there."

God chose us and made us from the Earth, just as diamonds are mined and sifted from the dirt.

With the "God chip" inside, He always knows where I am. He always knows what I am going through. With the "God chip" inside, the Holy Spirit is always able to give God a specific location of where I am in my "here," what's going on with me spiritually. Am I obedient or disobedient? Am I living in the truth or am I confused about the truth?

How to Be Me

Wholeness of life depends on each individual arriving at the place where he or she understands how each is made, wired, and how each goes about communicating his or her individuality in everyday living.

In essence, you live out of who you are; you live you. The most comfortable position you can be in is a place where you can just be yourself. There is no put on, no façade; you don't have to impress anybody. Simply, you live who you are. You know who you are—your gifts, your talents, your abilities. You know your purpose, and you get up every day and live your life. It is the most comfortable place in the world for a person to be. There is no pressure in living like that.

But what happens? Men and women damage by misuse and forfeit by disuse those talents and abilities not used for their original purpose. Sadly, people live a life God did not design for them, and they live it out of pressure or demand, or because they are forced into certain situations and circumstances.

God says, "I don't want you to ever give up on who I made you to be, because I have a purpose for you upon the earth and I want you to be who you are in your 'here.' I want you to live a life that expresses you."

Always God is calling you and me to a place, a "here." I can be fully alive in my "here," without restrictions or limitations. I can step into me. I can be released from any of the pressures of life, anything that demands I be someone who I am not. I can just be me.

God always has a purpose for your "here." You may detest it. You may not like it. You may be thinking you can't wait for this to be over, and you may be right. It may be the most difficult place you have ever lived. It may be a trying place for you, but God has a purpose for your "here." You wouldn't be in your "here" had God not permitted you to be there.

♦ Where am I? I am in my "here."

- What am I doing? I am living me. I am becoming who I am. I am living out my life. I am doing the thing that God put me on the earth to do.

The process of a diamond, as you know, is much like the process of our life. There's a process to the Diamond Life. God always has a plan for us. He knew exactly what He was doing when He created us, made us, and formed us from dirt.

The Frontier of Deepest Desire

Your calling and identity are found in your heart, written in the depths of your being, and are discovered when you enter the frontier of your deepest desires.

People usually like shallow living because shallow living doesn't demand much. It is so easy to live on the surface, skim by, slide by, by the skin of their teeth. They do not like going deep. They don't want to have deep conversations; they are afraid of deep relationships. They are a surface kind of people by nature.

But God says, "I am going to show you who you are. You don't know who you are, but I am going to challenge your identity out of you. You are more than you think you are. I will allow circumstances to suddenly appear in your life, and I will let you be driven to the frontier of your deepest desires."

In that moment, something begins to happen. You

never want to judge your "here" only by what you see on the surface. You might look around at your "here" and judge it by someone else's "here" and say to yourself, "I prefer that to this." People constantly do this. They are always comparing themselves with someone else. They are always looking at somebody else's life and saying, "They don't live as godly as I do and they seem to be more blessed than I am. What's the deal here?"

Don't judge your "here" by what you see. Don't judge your "here" by your disappointments. Don't judge your "here" by the provision, or lack of it, that you are experiencing. If you are where God wants you to be, you will never be without care and protection. Life is not a problem to be solved, as some people believe. Life is an adventure to be lived. I enjoy it when I am challenged. I can always find something good in my worst moments.

But, as it is in physical life, so it is in spiritual life. Sometimes when things don't go well, the tendency is to focus on the negatives. When you begin to see what's wrong with your life instead of what's right, you get depressed and feel oppressed. You see other people seemingly happy, and you are envious, almost angry. Why am I not happy as they are? They seem to have everything going for them. I don't have anything going for me.

Get your eyes on the fact that you actually woke up this morning. Do you know how many people around the world didn't wake up today? If today was normal, it was 153,000. But you are alive! You actually had breath to breathe. You actually had food to eat. You are in sync with what's going on around you. You are going to see people whom you love today. You are going to interact with them. You are going to interact with His Kingdom need.

Life has been arranged by God so that the only way it can be fully lived is by faith. If you try to live life any other way than by faith, you will be disappointed. You are going to have to believe in the moment you are in and believe God has a reason for you to be there. While you are there, there is protection and provision, no matter what's going on in your life.

The place God calls you is where your deepest desires intersect with a Kingdom need. God knows why He put you on earth. He knows how He made you. There is something inside you that must be revealed for the Kingdom to be perfected through you. You may not even recognize those desires within you. You may not have fully experienced those desires. You may not even go there and think about them, but they are there. God says, "I want something to happen that pulls on those deepest desires within you, and I want you to intersect with a Kingdom need. You will step into your moment." Your "here" will suddenly become the richest place you have ever been. You will be standing anchored in your "here" and you will hear the voice of God.

Do not compare your Diamond Life to someone else's Diamond Life. You never know where they are in the process.

It's Your Time

How long is it going to be before you step up and say, "I am going to occupy my 'here.' I am not doing what other people want me to do any longer, I am not doing what circumstance demands any longer; I am going to step into what God made me to be. I am stepping into my gifts and my talents and my abilities. I am stepping into my calling. I am stepping into my identity. I am stepping into my purpose and nothing is going to stop me. I have heard from God and I have a confirmation from God in my heart and I am moving into my "here" today"?

When you sojourn with God He is responsible for three important things:

Direction to your "there"
Provision for you "there"
Protection in the pursuit of your "there"

God says, "If you run with Me, if you sojourn with Me, if you take the route that I choose for you according to the way I have gifted you, here are three things that you can always count on from Me."

First, He will give you direction from your "here" to your "there."

If there is any subject people ask me about, it is *direction*. How do I know which route God wants me to take, where He wants me to go?

Secondly, God will give you *provision*. You are probably on the right path, because He gives provision for your "there." God will never send you somewhere that you don't have provision. Your "there" and your journey to your "there" will have the provision of God given to you as God wills it for your life.

Thirdly, God will give you *protection* to get you there. He protects. Have you realized that God often protects you from yourself? You may think of God as protecting you from other people.

I make decisions sometimes when I am not capable of making them, and in that moment, God speaks to me and tries to protect me from myself. He says, "I want to give you protection."

Just as a diamond has worth, your life has worth. God has instilled value into your life!

I go from a "here" to a "there" that He has chosen. He gives direction. He gives provision. He gives protection.

Your life is "bigger than you" when you live His purpose for you. It's more than you. It's greater than you. You are bigger than your life when you live His purpose. To live bigger than your life means to live the purpose of God for you.

What is your "Kingdom-worth"? I will ask the question two ways:

- ♦ What is your kingdom worth?
- ♦ Or, what is your Kingdom-worth?

Your Kingdom-worth is determined by the degree to which you invest yourself into His Kingdom.

- ♦ At any given time, how invested are you in the Kingdom of God?
- ♦ Or, conversely, how invested are you in the world?

People are always trying to receive from God what they believe they need, and God is always trying to receive from people what His Kingdom needs. He says, "I've given you Kingdom abilities and Kingdom talents. I've given you Kingdom gifts. I've given you Kingdom influence." He asks you:

How invested are you in My Kingdom with your Kingdom gifts and your Kingdom talents?

- ♦ How much of you is into my Kingdom?
- ♦ How much of your time?
- ♦ How much of your energy?

- ♦ How much of your resources?
- ♦ Am I really "Number One" on your list?
- ♦ Is my Kingdom coming on earth more important to you than your Kingdom coming on earth?

What About Attitude?

You determine how much God's purpose will be manifested inside your life by your attitude.

Get up every day and understand God made and equipped you. He placed you and He wants you to go out into the world doing what you love and loving what you do. That's purpose! That's the most beautiful life you can live. There is no more perfect life than that. If you are doing what you love and loving what you do, you are living your purpose. The place He has for you is unique to your journey, and the place He calls you to be is also unique. He said, "I have a place for you."

On this freeway of life, God continually rains on you and me, and continually lifts up you and me. He continually pours His spiritual energy into each one until finally it can be said, "It's worth it all!"

Personally, it doesn't make any difference what I have been through in my life. I don't have one day in my life that I want to delete. On my worst day, I knew things could get better. On my worst day, I knew heaven was concerned about my soul. I wouldn't trade one day of my life.

Wherever you are on your journey, I want you to know God knows where you are. He hasn't abandoned you and He has not forsaken you; He has a "there" for you.

Joseph Jaworski made a powerful statement: "I discovered that people are not really afraid of dying; they are afraid of never having lived, not ever having deeply considered their life's highest purpose and at least tried to make a difference in this world."

What is your purpose? You are here to make a difference. The world needs you.

There is no such thing as a wasted gift. God never created a life to be wasted. There is no such thing as a wasted talent. God put them all into the earth for a purpose. You and I have a reason to be here. You and I were born at the precise moment when God needed our life in the earth. You were born at the right time, not the wrong time. You might feel as if you are out of step sometimes, but you are not. You are here at the exact moment when God wanted you to be here.

God knows not only how to locate you (find you), but He also knows how to locate you (place you). Being at the right place at the right time brings you face to face with the right opportunities.

LIFE GEMS

From Chapter Five

You will never arrive at your "there" if you don't live in your "here."

You live out of who you are; you live you.

God will challenge your identity out of you.

The place God calls you is where your deepest desires intersect with a Kingdom need.

Your life is "bigger than you" when you live His purpose for you.

CHAPTER SIX

"Your" Certified Value

Living Your G.A.P.

A "certified" diamond is one accompanied by a certificate issued by a professional laboratory that clearly defines its cut, color, clarity, and carats. A certified diamond is likely to cost more than one without a certificate.

There's a choice to be made when you purchase your Diamond Life. The display case has hundreds of options. Do you want the best, the brightest, the most expensive? Are you willing to settle for the diamond that is still beautiful, but much less expensive?

Whether you think so or not, you deserve the best, and God wants the best for your life. He has your Diamond Life placed in the display case. He has designed the best life for us. He has certified and licensed a life for us that is perfect. He wrote our diamond certification papers even before we were bought.

Oh yes, you shaped me first inside, then out; you formed me in my mother's womb. I thank you, High God—you're breathtaking! Body and soul, I am marvelously made! I worship in adoration—what a creation! You know me inside and out, you know every bone in my body; you know exactly how I was made, bit by bit, how I was sculpted from nothing into something. Like an open book, you watched me grow from conception to birth; all the stages of my life were spread out before you, the days of my life all prepared before I'd even lived one day (Psalm 139: 13-16, MSG).

The Importance of Choice

Choice is the chisel with which you sculpt your life. Choices frame you, make you, form you; they shape your life. You become an artist by your choices. You design your life. You chisel your life.

The price of choice is responsibility. You must, at some point, take responsibility for your choice. From God's Word, here is what you see:

Choice is power.
Choice is at the center of your being.
The creative power of your life is in your choices.
You can, by your choices, create.

I will discuss this at greater length in another chapter. This means you need to stop complaining about what your life looks like. People complain about their lives, when in reality their lives consist of their choices and if they want their lives to change, they must change their choices.

When you see anything that's alive, vibrant, and healthy, you are looking at something as God made it. You are looking at how beautiful something can be. On the other hand, when you see a living thing that is wounded or hurting, or has been weakened, bruised, and battered, you are witnessing how ugly life can become. All around us you see those examples. You see things of beauty that God has made, and it just takes your breath away.

The beauty or ugliness of any life is simply determined by how a person chooses to process the things that happen to him- or herself. No one can choose my life to be beautiful. No one can choose for my life to be ugly. No one can make my life beautiful. No one can make my life ugly. It doesn't matter what happens *to* me; it matters what happens *inside* of me. How do I handle it? How do I process it? How does it affect me in my daily living?

The Power of Memory

Within the soul is something called "memory," which records the events of life. Everyone has a memory. Things written on the brain are not erased, even though sometimes it would be desirable if they were.

The late commentator, Andy Rooney, made us laugh when he expounded his humorous theory that at a certain age the brain gets full. In order to permit more input into the memory, the brain has to let some of its content leak out, and that's why older people can't remember as well as younger people. We smile at the idea; however, the fact is, all the memories are indelibly imprinted. They're still there.

Psychologists point out that everything a person has ever seen, heard, or known is recorded in the brain. One may not have the greatest power of recall, but the memories are all written there, and at some point or another, something makes a demand on the recollection button and a good memory or a bad memory comes right back to the front.

In California, there are sequoia trees and redwood trees whose rings reveal their developmental history, year by year. Some of the trees are as many as 4,000 years old, and some of them are so huge that they reach nearly 400 feet tall. They are so wide at the bottom that developers have cut a hole in one of the trees large enough for a car to drive through. Every year the tree lives, it forms a ring and the ring tells the developmental story of the great redwood and sequoia trees. The rings are different on the trees. Each tree has its own unique set of rings.

If a redwood tree is set afire, 80 percent of it can burn up, and the 20 percent left will regenerate its life and it will become a healthier tree. No matter what happens to them, the trees keep on living. Those rings form every year. A botanist could look at that tree and immediately know its history. For example, a narrow ring would indicate a particular year of drought or a wider-than-usual ring might signal an abundance of rain. In another year, you might look at that ring and it will tell you the tree caught on fire and was burned, or it was struck by lightning. In that moment, the botanist would understand and know what happened to the tree. These rings tell the story.

These rings are like the thumbprint that tells something about you, identifies you. Each individual has a story to tell. It's in your thumbprint. What happens in your life, the way you live, the things that have happened to you, the things you suffer, all mark you, scar you in some way.

There is a history of life; there is a story of life written on the inside of each person. This history lies embedded in the heart of the tree, in the heart of the person.

It is the same with everyone. It doesn't matter who you are, there is a developmental story within your heart, your inner being covered by a protective bark, a protective mask, to prevent anyone from seeing too deeply inside. There are scars of ancient and painful hurts, or stains, or blights on your life. All of the things that ever happened to you are recorded within. They deeply and profoundly affect your feelings, they affect your relationships, your actions, the words you speak, and how you live your life, whether you are up or down, whether you are in or out. The inconsistencies of your life are all revealed from within.

Processing Your Hurt

But not only that, the story of your life—the things that have happened to you—affect how you see God. It affects how you interpret who God is, it affects how you see life, and it affects how you see other people. Even how you see yourself is determined by the story of your life.

Never allow for some disappointment, some moment of pain or hurt, to become an idol in your life. An incident that profoundly affects you in a negative way could become something you bow down to. You surrender to it. You can't master it. You can't get over it. You can't overcome it and it becomes an idol in your life. It determines how you live your life. It determines what your feelings are towards other people.

The Bible says that there is no wound too deep inside and there is no hurt too great that God cannot heal it. God sent His Son, Jesus Christ, to be the Healer—not just to heal physical infirmities, but to reach inside and heal the spirit and take care of the wounds of the heart.

The Bible declares, "He [Jesus Christ] Himself took our infirmities" (Matthew 8:17, AMP). He bore *infirmities*. I want you to keep the word "infirmities" in your mind and think about this word with me. I want you to see the power of His Word. Jesus bore my infirmities. The Word also reveals that the Spirit comes along and helps my infirmities, identified in this Bible translation as "weakness."

Likewise the Spirit helps us in our weakness. For we do not know what to pray for as we ought, but the Spirit himself intercedes for us with groanings too deep or words (Romans 8:26, ESV).

Helps is a word that inspires the picture of a nurse who aids us in the healing process. After a wound or an affliction, which has been treated by a doctor or by medicine, the nurse comes along and aids in the process. The doctor comes alongside to begin the healing. The nurse comes in after the medication has been dispensed, after the disinfectant has been administered. The nurse takes hold of a suffering hand and says, "I will lead you to the other side of your infirmities."

God says to you, "I know your heart is going to be broken; it's going to be crushed. I know you are going to have wounds in your heart, but this is the very place where the Holy Spirit resides. He will come along beside you as a nurse to take your hand and nurse you through your moment. He takes you through it to the other side of it."

> **When we long for life without difficulties, remind us that oaks grow strong in contrary winds and diamonds are made under pressure.**
>
> —PETER MARSHALL

It is not His desire that you camp out in your pain. He wants you to make a decision not to live there. He says, "I want you to understand that this is a journey. I am going to take you through the journey of your trial."

God has a life design that no one can create a match for. God wants you to choose His life. He won't force you, but He wants you to see His good intent when He created you.

Discovering Your G.A.P.

Have you ever wondered who you are and for what purpose you are on the planet? Everything that exists on earth and in the universe has a specific God-assigned purpose (G.A.P.).

Your G.A.P. births hope and creates enthusiasm and passion. Without purpose, life has no heart. Living the life you were created for is dependent on your becoming who you were born to be and doing what you were born to do. Purpose is simply our "role" discovered. Purpose is found in the reason for your circumstances. It's behind your objective in life. There is nothing more energizing than to know your G.A.P. and to do it.

Living your G.A.P. brings fulfillment. Within each of

us, there is a cry coming forth which says, "I want to live; I want to come alive. I want to be whom I was born to be." Without purpose, life lacks meaning. Purpose is the key to life. Living on purpose is the primary goal of every person who desires significance. Your purpose defines your existence.

When you live your G.A.P., your life is filled with achievement and production.

Purpose is:

- ♦ The why for the creation of anything.
- ♦ The fulfilled desire that caused the production.
- ♦ The destiny that prompts the journey.
- ♦ The hope for the achievement.
- ♦ The reason for the pursuit.

You were created for more than existence or survival, and for more than success; you were created for significance, and for living your G.A.P. To limit who you are is to limit who you will become. When God looks at you, He sees things everyone else ignores. Do you see the "you" that God sees?

If you know where you came from and you know where you are going, you will never have to worry about where you are.

To live your G.A.P., you must rid yourself of every hindrance that is interfering with or holding you back. Too often we allow others to define what is best for our lives. Some allow their work to define their sense of purpose.

To live your G.A.P., take your ideas and turn them into imagination; then take your imagination and duplicate it physically. Write it down. Let it become a plan of action. When you do this you become a visionary working on a mission. When your dream becomes a vision and your vision becomes your mission, you begin to live a life of purpose.

You cannot be successful without being fulfilled. You cannot be fulfilled without living on purpose. Success can only be defined by purpose and measured by obedience. Success is not what you have achieved compared to what others have achieved, but what you have achieved compared to your created purpose. Living on purpose is the difference between being busy and being effective. Don't waste your time doing the wrong thing. Refuse to allow activity without progress to dominate your existence.

Living on purpose keeps you settled on the path. Living on purpose will influence whom you spend time with. Living on purpose will influence and determine your priorities.

Every person has a specific position and purpose in the plan of God for the world. Every one of us is being strategically positioned by God in some manner, some way, some fashion. We actually determine the importance of our position by our yielding to God, by our willingness to obey Him, by our willingness to surrender to Him.

Your DNA—your gifts, talents, abilities, position, your likes, your dislikes, your personality, what turns you on, what turns you off, motivates you, un-motivates you—this is what makes you "you." This is how God specifically designed you to perform the assignment He purposed for you.

He knew what He wanted you to do, who He wanted you to become, and He set it up so you would become that person. Then when you experience your purpose, you come alive inside and are fully motivated and activated in the Kingdom purpose. You get excited about it and every day is a great day—a day of joy, a day of energy, and a day of living. You can't wait to get up and get started. I maintain that God put each of us here and then said, "I have a place for you, a position, a passion, purpose."

You don't have to struggle to get there. You don't have to move anyone else out of the way. Do you realize that God is the Perfect Chess Master? He knows which piece is needed, where and when, as He strategically positions our lives for greatness.

If you really want to be alive that means you've got to take responsibility for your life. You must embrace the moment. In doing so, you open yourself up to become everything God created you to be. All of us have seen people who are half-activated, and those who are not activated at all. Determine you will be fully activated into the purpose God intended for you when He put you on this earth.

Someone has suggested a self-inventory that looks like this.

- ♦ Always be where you are.
- ♦ Where you are, determines who you meet.
- ♦ Who you meet, determines how you think.
- ♦ How you think, determines what you do.
- ♦ What you do, determines your destiny.

Always be in your moment, or you could miss your life.

The Diamond Life is the life you were intended to live. The Diamond Life will take you to a place where you begin to see what you are worth, what you have to offer this world. You will discover "you" through the process of human certification—how you respond to life. Only when we make our purposes God's purposes do we discover the certified life. Like every diamond, we can be certified too.

True friends are like diamonds, precious and rare.
False friends are like leaves, found everywhere.

—ANONYMOUS

Certification qualifies us for our purpose. With that comes assurance, confidence, and a boldness of life. Certification is where you find "you." You are then freed up to live your purpose. The certification process brings you face to face with your true value. It is your G.A.P. that certifies your value. When you live your purpose, you become invincible. You are bigger than your life. Every diamond has its own unique worth, thus every diamond has its own unique value. Once properly certified, a diamond can never be de-certified; so, with you. You can never be less than you were certified to be. The mark of certification in The Diamond Life is the favor of God. Focus on God's purpose for you and you will be fulfilled. Living your G.A.P. inspires passion, sustains energy, and unleashes creativity.

You are God's "work of art" and you are certified!

LIFE GEMS

From Chapter Six

God designed you for His best life.

The choices you make make you.

There is a story of life written on the inside of you.

Never camp out in your pain.

Always live in your G.A.P.

You cannot be successful without being fulfilled.

Always embrace your moment.

CHAPTER SEVEN

The Cost of "Your" Diamond Life

The Price is Right

The Christian life is not always easy. There will be choices to make, but in the end those choices—if you make them for the Kingdom—will be the best choices you make in your life.

"I call heaven and earth to witness this day against you that I have set before you life and death, the blessings and the curses; therefore choose life, that you and your descendants may live" (Deuteronomy 30:19, AMP).

The Kohinoor diamond is the most valuable diamond in the world. Kohinoor means "Mountain of Light" in Persian. It's a 105-carat stone that originated at the Golconda mine in the Andhra Pradesh state of India. How much is worth? It's never been given an estimate; it's just referred to as "priceless."

The Sancy, a vivid yellow diamond of 55 carats, is also without price. The most valuable diamond that has been sold, the Star of Africa, is valued at $400 million. They only became valuable because they endured the process of heat, pressure, and time. You, like these precious stones, have infinite worth. In your case, your actions and choices will determine your value.

Choices Make You

You are who you constantly choose to be and what you repeatedly choose to do.

Every single day of your life—whoever you are, wherever you are, whatever color your skin is, whichever culture you live in, wherever you came from, or what planet you live on—you make choices. What you do is what you choose to do. It doesn't make any difference who you are, your life is filled with choices, decisions that subsequently make your life. The choices you make make you.

Two choices, two rules that you make in life govern the way you live.

Choice Number One:
You can choose to be less than God created you to be.

You can make a choice say, "I will limit my life. I will live less than I was created to be." The make-up of your spirit, soul, and body, the way that God constituted you with gifts, talents, and abilities help determine your success. Everything you are—your intellect, your abilities, your wants, your likes, your dislikes, your desires—helps to create your success, but you can choose to be less than God created you to be. In fact, it is possible for you to make this choice without choosing, if you just live without making a decision.

Choice Number Two:
You can choose to be all God created you to be.

You can actually go above and beyond what you are capable of, according to the Word of God. The presence of God and the gifting of God will take you beyond your natural abilities, and you will be able to accomplish more than you can dream or think. You shall be able to do exceeding, abundantly above all that you ask or think according to the power of God that's released in you by your choices.

Concerning your choices, life has two rules:

Rule Number One:
Your choices have consequences.

Every choice has a consequence. Every choice you make produces something. Something comes of that choice. A direction in life comes out of that choice.

Rule Number Two:
You are responsible for your choices.

Personally, here is what I know: At any given time, my life is exactly what I've chosen it to be. I have had people argue this point with me for 20 years and people who will continue to argue that point, but it is the absolute truth. I can't choose what happens to me, but I can choose what happens within me. I can determine how I will function relative to what life dishes out to me. No one can determine my choices as to my options about what happens to me. I have the power and the privilege from God to do that.

Life's greatest education comes from consistently making wise choices. If you want to be informed, smart, intelligent, and you want to live life in a powerful, effective, influential fashion, then remember to make wise choices, which continually educate your life. Making right choices is life's greatest weapon of empowerment. You can't be more empowered than to make right choices. They move you closer to being the person God created you to be. Right choices move you up; they move you forward. They help you, nurture you, and enrich you.

- ♦ Do your daily life choices reflect that you are choosing life?
- ♦ Have you chosen to live by the plan and the purpose of God, or your own plan and purpose?

- Do your choices make your Diamond Life more or less valuable?

If you live by your plan and go the way of your *flesh*, you may live in comfort. (Flesh is the term used in the Bible sometimes as a synonym for *body*. In that sense, it is neutral, not evil. Since the flesh may be weak, however, it may become the arena in which sin entrenches itself. It is in this sense the term is used here.) The flesh loves comfort, ease.

The flesh wants to sit outside when it's warm and drink iced tea or lemonade, but if you really want to make the most of the weather, you will start walking, running, or jogging rather than just sitting. You will make a right choice. You will choose against comfort in order that you may lengthen your days and live the life God chose for you.

The Paths of Choice

Let me walk you down a few of the paths people can choose in life.

Some have chosen to travel down *Addiction Avenue*. They abuse substances, not just illegal drugs, but legal drugs. In the process of abusing substances, they abuse their own body, soul, and spirit and this reduces the value of their Diamond Life.

Some have chosen to walk through *Ego Estate*. They are full of pride. If you make a choice to be prideful, pride goes before a fall. If you are prideful, full of boasting and arrogance, you will fall. *Ego Estate* does not improve your bottom line.

Others have chosen *Things Trail.* They live their whole lives to accumulate money, goods, things, toys—unadulterated materialism. That's what their life is about. They just want to keep accumulating. They kill themselves working to accrue things. A man in New York City worked 18 to 20 hour days to amass a fortune, only to eventually kill himself. For what? It makes no sense. He got caught up in materialism. There is no value in the accumulation of material things, but you can store up treasures in Heaven.

Some will travel down *Immorality Interstate*. They are involved in sexual sins, adultery, fornication, or homosexuality. You cannot live in sexual sin and please God; you are unable to live the life you are called to live. Sexual sins will take away from the years of your life and morality will bring wholeness in spirit, soul, and body.

Some will choose *Hate Highway.* If you hate, if you have anger, you are killing your internal organs. Anger imprisons you. You are destroying your body. You have chosen death. Get rid of your anger. Forgiveness is the greatest antidote to anger; it brings freedom, release and pardon.

Still, others will choose *Lethargic Lane*. They are apathetic about everything. They are not upset about sin. They live an indifferent life. God didn't design anyone to live an apathetic life. God is not into lethargy and laziness. They value of The Diamond Life is found in hope, energy, and positive expressions.

Here lies the problem: when you choose a path, you choose a destiny, since every path leads somewhere. When you make a choice, you've chosen a path. Will that path lead to increase or in some way diminish your Diamond Life?

God's purpose for you remains steadfast no matter what path you choose in life. Whichever path you go down, or how badly you live, or what sin you are involved in, God will never give up on your purpose. He has a plan to increase and add value to your Diamond Life.

Sin, disobedience, or self-will has the power to send you on a detour away from the direction God wills you to travel, but nothing that happens in your life ever takes God by surprise. He always has a plan to redirect your path and move you in the way you ought to be walking. His purpose is never hindered by your past bad choices. He does not hold your past sins before you as some think He does.

"If You, Lord, should keep account of and treat [us according to our] sins, O Lord, who could stand? But there is forgiveness with You [just what man needs], that You may be reverently feared and worshiped" (Psalm 130:3, 4, AMP).

His plan is still in effect. He can still redeem you. Did you know that God can redeem you and get more out of you in one year than you can get out of your life in 50 years?

Choosing His Purpose: Priceless

When you choose God's purposes, which are often beyond your capacities, you will discover His provision. It's just clear and simple. God said, "I give you everything back. You don't get cheated because you went down the wrong path. The Enemy cannot steal from you the plan God has for your life. Things may distract you, but nothing hinders God from perfecting His will in your life. I give God "who" I am and He gives me "who" He made me to be.

When I make a choice, I've chosen a path, and then I must answer these three questions:

- Am I willing to hang onto that choice until I get to the end of the path?
- Where does the path lead me?
- What is the consequence of traveling the path?

Each path has a destination, a payoff.

I see people making choices every day that are killing them, and I don't understand. Should you say to them:

- ♦ Do you want to live?
- ♦ They would say yes.
- ♦ Do you want to live a long life?
- ♦ They would say yes.
- ♦ But, why are you making these choices?
- ♦ Well, you don't understand what happened to me.

No, you don't understand what God has said about you. God said, "Choose life or choose death." Black, white; one, two; A, B. There are not many choices here; there are two:

Enter through the narrow gate; for wide is the gate and spacious and broad is the way that leads away to destruction, and many are those who are entering through it. But the gate is narrow (contracted by pressure) and the way is straightened and compressed that leads away to life, and few are those who find it (Matthew 7:13-14, AMP).

I want you to see the power of choice, and how God speaks to us in a message about how life is lived. Two different choices are presented to us. There is the broad gate, the broad way that leads to destruction. There is the straight, narrow gate that leads to life. That is a lonely road sometimes and that is the price you pay for the cost of The Diamond Life. One of the great discoveries in life is when we accept that we must become limited in order to truly experience life's unlimited potential.

Life is all about the choices you and I make, and those choices will produce winners or losers on a day-by-day basis. Understand the power of this truth. No one can make you a loser without your permission. You have to choose to be a loser before you can be a loser in this life. That's how God set life up. It's impossible for somebody, some company, some organization, to make you a loser unless you choose to be a loser. If you choose to win, no one can stop you. Winners must always pay the price, bear the cost, and accept the discipline that will lead them into The Diamond Life.

> **Two roads diverged in a wood, and I—I took the one less traveled by, And that has made all the difference.**
>
> —ROBERT FROST

Robert Frost wrote a beautiful poem, "The Road Not Taken," that has different shades of meaning. In the poem, the writer approaches a fork in the road and wrestles with which direction he should take. Here is what he concluded:

"I took the one that nobody was traveling on," he said, "I didn't go for the ordinary, I didn't go for the regular, I took the other one, and that has made all the difference." So here is the analogy: Your life will consist of the sum total of your choices and decisions. Whoever you are at any given moment is because of the choices you have made previously.

Maybe in some of those choices, you didn't feel as if you had a choice, and sometimes, without making the choice, you did.

Jesus comes crashing into our world, offering a dramatically powerful choice in Matthew 7. He says choose the narrow, straight way which leads to life, or the wide, broad way which leads to destruction.

Every single day you will make a choice as to which road you are going to travel. Proverbs 14:12 states,

> *There is a way which seems right to a man*
> *and appears straight before him, but at the*
> *end of it is the way of death*
> *(AMP).*

The 19th century poet John Oxenham wrote a poem called "The Way," in which he declared,

> **To every man there openeth**
> **A Way, and Ways, and a Way,**
> **And the High Soul climbs the High Way,**
> **And the Low Soul gropes the Low,**
> **And in between, on the misty flats,**
> **The rest drift to and fro.**
> **But to every man there openeth**
> **A High Way, and a Low.**
> **And every man decideth**
> **The way his soul shall go.**
>
> —JOHN OXENHAM

This matter of "drifting to and fro" isn't an option that continues indefinitely. A choice *must* be made, and if it is the right choice, the sooner the better.

The will of God is a path you choose. You don't go to God and say, "I'll add your will onto my life." The will of God for your life is actually a path that you choose to walk. It's a road. It's a way. You actually have to choose His path, and His will becomes the path of your life.

Ultimately for all men and women, it is an inescapable choice. You are going to choose one of two paths, so examine both of them. Listen to the wisdom of Jesus when he admonished everyone to count the cost.

> *Don't think I've come to make life cozy. I've come to cut—make a sharp knife-cut between son and father, daughter and mother, bride and mother-in-law—cut through these cozy domestic arrangements and free you for God. Well-meaning family members can be your worst enemies. If you prefer father or mother over me, you don't deserve me. If you prefer son or daughter over me, you don't deserve me. If you don't go all the way with me, through thick and thin, you don't deserve me. If your first concern is to look after yourself, you'll never find yourself. But if you forget about yourself and look to me, you'll find both yourself and me*
> *Matthew 10:34-39 (MSG).*

First, there is a pathway that is broad, spacious, and roomy. The crowds are on that one and it's the way of lax morality. It's a way of tolerance; it's a way of permissiveness that has no curbs and no boundaries of thought or conduct. It is the way of least resistance.

Let me use street language to explain it. Anything goes. No boundaries, no curbs to the thinking process or even the actions, the conduct. It is just, "Do what feels good." It is engaging in whatever behavior satisfies you at the moment. Just make your momentary decisions and live for the excitement of your flesh. The crowd is on this road, which ultimately leads to destruction, and they will go with you. It would be easy to go down this road because you will always find people to go down this road with you. It's the crowded way and the cheap way-or so it appears. And in the end, it will cost you your life.

God's message about this direction is simply, "Don't choose the popular road of the prevailing culture; choose the other path—the Christian counterculture. Take the road less traveled, the "Free Way." This path costs you everything; it demands complete surrender-spirit, soul, body-but the payback is huge.

What will happen? Your payback will be an abundant life. You will have overflowing life. You can walk out of your addictions. You can walk out of your pain; you can walk out of your suffering. You can walk out of your depression; you can walk out of your oppression. You can walk out of anything that the Enemy has done to take away from your Diamond Life. You can say no to it. You can walk toward that straight gate and that narrow way.

The imagery is beautiful. God says, "Wide is the gate and broad is the way that leads to destruction." The moment you walk through the wide gate, that road closes down and you get pressured and compressed by sin. You get beaten up and squeezed. But the moment you walk through the straight gate leading to the narrow way, once you are on the narrow way, it broadens out into the greatest liberty you have ever experienced. There you feel the freedom to pursue your destiny.

Your destiny is The Diamond Life. It assumes the role as the beautiful finished diamond. The past-the dirt, the burden, the scars, the hard times, the rejection, the pain, the obstacles-is now gone. You realize you are more than you have become. The Diamond Life offers promise, trust-a trust that can't be mistaken for anything else.

You realize you are more than you have become. With a certified diamond there comes a trust factor-authenticity, value, clarity, and weight-which has been proven. The trust factor is so vital in the creativity of a Diamond Life. You must be able to trust the value God has assigned to your Diamond Life because His price is always right.

LIFE GEMS

From Chapter Seven

Never choose to be less than who God created you to be.

Your choices have consequences.

When you choose a path, you choose a destiny.

God will never give up on your purpose.

Your life will consist of the sum total of your choices and decisions.

Your destiny is The Diamond Life.

"Your" Secured Wealth

The Beauty of Your Riches

Once mined, once polished,
the diamond has a destiny to be displayed.
Just so, you—living The Diamond Life—are on
display, not to be admired, but to serve,
to complete your God-given destiny.

For as the sky soars high above earth,
so the way I work surpasses the way you work,
and the way I think is beyond the way you think.
Just as rain and snow descend from the skies
and don't go back until they've watered the earth,
Doing their work of making things grow and blossom,
producing seed for farmers and food for the hungry,
So will the words that come out of my mouth
not come back empty-handed.
They'll do the work I sent them to do,
they'll complete the assignment I gave them
(Isaiah 55:10-11, MSG).

Every life comes with a G.A.P. which involves a God-assignment. It is the living of your purpose and the completion of your assignment that brings you to your destination. You are destined to arrive at a place of immeasurable worth and influence in God's Kingdom.

CHAPTER EIGHT

Trusting "Your" Diamond Value

The Comfort of Security

You will never understand trust until you trust.

What causes you to trust the value of a diamond? Because of this certification process, you can trust the value of a diamond. As you interact with God, and discover your Kingdom purpose, the life-process creates trust. You learn to trust God on the basis of two things: His Word and your experience with Him. The process creates trust.

Perhaps one of the most neglected principles of life can be summed up in one word: trust.

The Trust Process

Government, commerce, business, education, society, nations, families, universities, financial institutions, and marriages—all are dependent upon this powerful principle of life. And these institutions could never function if not for trust.

All of creation loudly proclaims the message of trust and everything God created was meant to establish the principle of trust upon the Earth. When spring brings the greening of the planet, for example, the air is fresh and alive with oxygen. The sun deposits heat, light, and energy. Trees and shrubs, flowers and plants, even the grass gives life by producing oxygen.

Everything God created gives and makes deposits into human lives. Thus life is sustained and maintained. No one ever worries whether the sun will shine, whether plants will grow, or whether the planets will continue in their orbits. In that sense, all have learned to trust God.

Learning to trust and living a life of trust is an absolute "must" if you want to experience The Diamond Life. In the Kingdom of God, the word "trust" is an important and powerful word. It is upon the basis of trust that any relationship with God is built.

But what does it mean to trust God? Some people might say, "To trust God means you ought to have confidence in Him." And they are correct. Others might say, "It means you ought to have faith in God." And that, also, would be right. But to me, the word "trust" conveys much more. I think it is important for us to understand the depth of meaning of this particular biblical word.

The root of the word *trust* means "safety; refuge;

security; boldness; confidence." God wants you to know that He is a God of security. You can run to Him. You can submit yourself to His care without worry or frustration. You can place yourself in His capable, reliable, and dependable hands.

Panic is the opposite of confidence. And quite often, God's people panic when circumstances arise that present a challenge to them. Often, they do not view God as a refuge. They forget that He is mindful of their plights and situations. But God knows everything. He knows what time they went to bed last night. He knows what they had for breakfast three days after their 16th birthdays. They may forget things, but God never forgets, unless He chooses to forget. (Remember, He forgets the sins of a forgiven person.) God sees everything, knows everything, and remembers everything.

God, investigate my life; get all the facts firsthand.
I'm an open book to you;
even from a distance, you know what I'm thinking.
You know when I leave and when I get back;
I'm never out of your sight.
You know everything I'm going to say
before I start the first sentence.
I look behind me and you're there,
then up ahead and you're there, too—
your reassuring presence, coming and going.

This is too much, too wonderful—
I can't take it all in!
Oh yes, you shaped me first inside, then out;
you formed me in my mother's womb.
I thank you, High God—you're breathtaking!
Body and soul, I am marvelously made!
I worship in adoration—what a creation!
You know me inside and out,
you know every bone in my body;
You know exactly how I was made, bit by bit,
how I was sculpted from nothing into something.
Like an open book, you watched me grow from
conception to birth; all the stages of my life were
spread out before you, The days of my life all
prepared before I'd even lived one day
(Psalm 139:1-6, 13-16, MSG).

No detail escapes the knowledge of God, and that fact alone ought to bring us great hope. But if you are going to trust the Lord, then you need to understand that biblical trust involves confidence and security.

To trust is to be secure and to live without fear.

I think that is a fascinating definition of trust: security without fear. You were born to live The Diamond Life. God has committed himself to you becoming valuable to yourself, others, and to His Kingdom. Listen to His words:

As soon as Babylon's seventy years are up and not a day before, I'll show up and take care of you as I promised and bring you back home. I know what I'm doing. I have it all planned out—plans to take care of you, not abandon you, plans to give you the future you hope for. When you call on me, when you come and pray to me, I'll listen Jeremiah 29:10-12 (MSG).

Security Without Fear

He has done everything possible to secure your trust without fear in living The Diamond Life. Life is filled with fear. It doesn't matter where you go. It doesn't matter where you look, life is filled with fear. Turn on your television tonight and you will see news items that cause fear. Read the headlines in today's newspaper and you will discover concerns that breed fear. Study politics and you will observe matters that will make you afraid. Study religion and you will learn insights that will shake your confidence. The same is true of medicine, law, business, finance, education, and every other endeavor of man. If it's part of the world, part of the world system, it will breed fear in the human heart, because there is risk in every endeavor and every relationship.

Terrorists strike innocent victims without warning. Young girls contract AIDS from their dentists. High school athletes drop dead of heart attacks after practice sessions. Senior citizens are unexpectedly killed by drunk drivers.

And children are slain in acts of random violence at daycare centers. In this world, everyday life generates fear.

In The Diamond Life, trust will cause you to come to a place of security without fear. You will come to a place where you won't worry about what *might* happen to you. After all, worry is nothing more than the agony created by thoughts of what might happen, not what is happening. And God can give you peace and confidence in the face of any possibility. You can actually come to a place in your spiritual life where you can face a terminal illness and stand secure in the Lord without fear. You can come to a place in your life where you can face financial catastrophe and stand secure in the Lord without fear. It doesn't matter what you face and what you fear; you can put your trust in the Lord Jesus Christ and actually be secure in Him without any fear.

Nothing inspires God to action as trust does. God regularly moves Heaven and Earth for those people who dared to trust Him, believe Him, and lean upon Him in confidence.

God says, "I want you to be secure in Me. I don't want you to go to bed worried at night. I don't want you to pace the floor during the twilight hours, searching for answers that just aren't there. I want you to have the confidence that I can take care of you and your situation. I want you to know I love you, that you're important to Me. I'm going to do something about your situation. If you will hold on to Me, if you will put your confidence in Me, then you will come to that place of being secure in Me without any fear whatsoever."

God has committed true riches to your care. The Diamond Life is a deposit of wealth and truth that has been entrusted to you and me to increase the value of our lives, just as the diamond's worth is caused by the earth's heat, pressure, and time. In effect, you have become a "trustee" or "steward" of the Word of God. (A steward is one who is assigned and trusted to manage the belongings of another.) Remember, diamonds come out of a unique process designed by God. Jewelers have learned to trust that uniqueness of production. Likewise, your Diamond Life is uniquely produced by God in a trust relationship through heat, pressure, and time of your life. But God would have you know that faithfulness is the most important virtue that can be found in a trustee or steward. In fact, the Bible declares that there is a direct correlation between your faithfulness and God's willingness to trust you with greater things.

Trust is a two-way street.

In The Diamond Life, I am a trustee of the deposit God has put into me. Every person is purposed to live a destiny in the kingdom of God. There was never a person born who lacked a living purpose. Every man, every woman, every boy, every girl! It does not matter who you are. You were intended for the purposes of the Kingdom of God. God has a plan for your life and a plan to accomplish that destiny. And His plan is very simple and trustworthy. He says: "I will make deposits." After all, it's His deposits that made the diamond.

Why does God deposit His unchangeable word in the lives of mortal men and women? Because God wants us to be stewards and trustees of His word. He wants every voice in the land to speak for the gospel of Jesus Christ, and He wants every ear to hear that word. He wants every soul to understand His good news. He wants everyone to receive a deposit from Him so others can see the value of the deposit. God intends for the whole earth to be filled with the beauty, knowledge, and value of His wisdom.

The spirit of the world understands this divine process, so it makes its own deposits into your lives; at least, it attempts to. In order to counteract the work of the spirit of the world that forever bombards us with its own influences and devices through its tantalizing appeal, its gripping power, and attacks, you and I have a choice to make in life. You get to choose which deposits you want to accept. You can accept the deposits of God into your life: His mercy, His grace, His blessings, His power, His anointing, His glory, and His gifts. Or you can choose the immediate gratifications and easy pathways of the world's substitutes. The choice is yours! One can be trusted to bring you into your Diamond Life, while the other will for sure crush and destroy you.

God desires more for us than existence, survival; He desires more for us than success. His desire for us is significance.

Every morning, when I get up, there are two beings waiting to make deposits into my account. And if I continually choose the right path, if I choose to accept heavenly deposits into my account, God will entrust me with even more things. He will entrust me with spiritual greatness in all areas of life. In other words, in the Kingdom of God, the rich get richer and the poor get poorer. Now that's compound interest in its highest form!

The Reward of Trust

Luke 16:11 says, "So if you have not been trustworthy in handling worldly wealth, who will trust you with true riches?"

God entrusts us with increasing responsibilities and increasing blessings. But the passage also makes it clear that material wealth is the least important thing that God will entrust to us. Material wealth (money) is the lowest level of responsibility, so it is God's proving ground for higher levels of trust (true riches). Money is not the highest level of trust; His word is the highest level of trust. The love of God is the greatest treasure and experience in your Diamond Life. Material things are worth nothing when compared to the presence and the companionship and the power of Almighty God.

According to Luke, unfaithfulness in the use of money and possessions disqualifies a person from true heavenly wealth. In other words, Jesus is saying that if you don't know how to use your money and your possessions—if you don't know how to honor God with them—then you will never be entrusted with the true heavenly riches. That's a powerful statement! That would shake me up if I didn't contribute to God's Kingdom. I know from this statement that if God cannot depend upon me to give back to Him that which is already His, then how can He possibly trust me with real blessings and real favor?

> **Life is God's gift to you; what you do with that life is your gift back to God.**
>
> **—LEO BUSCAGLIA**

A person may think his life and his possessions are his own. But the Bible says that if you are the Lord's, then you are a steward of the Lord's blessings. You are a steward, therefore, of the possessions God has entrusted to you. You are a steward of the life God has entrusted to you. A diamond's value is assigned on the basis of its response to the elements of the earth. Your Diamond Life is based on your response to His deposits in your life. If you were to make a diamond, you would probably never think to start with a lump of coal, but God did. Thus, you can always trust His deposits and decisions into your life.

- What are you doing with your life?
- What are you doing with what you have been given?
- What are you doing with the deposits God has entrusted to your care?

Truly, He makes deposits on a daily basis, an hourly basis, a minute-by-minute basis into your life.

Actually, all that I possess has been given to me by God, and God has trusted me with all of it. I am a holder and steward of what is His. If I handle my life and my possessions badly, it demonstrates that I am not fit to be trusted with the responsibilities that will come in the new heavens and the new earth. In the life that is to come, earth's deposits determine our future service in the Kingdom. And the Bible tells me that responsibilities are going to be given to those people who trusted God and who were faithful with what He entrusted to them. When that time comes, you will be given responsibilities based on how you handled your life here on earth. Did you live The Diamond Life or one of your making? Did you trust His deposits or did you make your own?

Your ROI – Return on Investment

This principle of responsible stewardship applies to my possessions, but it also applies to my talents and my time, as well. If I can sing, then God will hold me accountable for that deposit He has made into my life. If I teach, then God will hold me accountable for that deposit. I must study to perfect the ability, work to share it with others, and pray over it diligently. Whatever I am, God gave that to me. So it's already His. It belongs to Him already. He wants to know: "Can I trust you to give that back to Me? I'm going to give it to you. I'm going to entrust it to you. Now what will you do with it?"

But you will only do something with your time, your talents, and your treasure if you view those things as divine deposits in your life. God expects you to steward the time, talents, and wealth He has entrusted to you. He also expects you to use those things wisely and protect them for Him. And He expects to get something back for His investment. That's the law of sowing and reaping. Into every person He has sown a Diamond Life looking for a ROI-return on investment.

Suppose for a moment that I deposit $1,000 in a mutual fund. Suppose that, at the end of the year, the fund has earned 25 percent on its investment. I should expect to have $1,250 in my account (the $1,000 that was originally invested and $250 in interest). But suppose I attempt to get my money, and I learn that nobody did anything with it. My money had been left in the manager's desk drawer all year, earning nothing at all. How do you suppose I would feel? Do you suppose I would feel happy? Do you suppose I would feel confident in that individual's ability to manage greater amounts of my money? Absolutely not! Does that help you understand how God feels when you mismanage what is His?

Once again, God says: "I am going to trust you with the deposit of gifts, talents, and abilities. I am going to trust you with certain truths about Me. I am going to trust you with the power of my Word, with material resources, with spiritual gifts, and with the treasure of time. Now, show Me what you are made of. Use what I give you to prove everything I could ever want to know about your character, your priorities, and your work ethic. Show me your Diamond Life by your living."

> **There are two kinds of people:**
> **those who say to God, "Thy will be done,"**
> **and those to whom God says,**
> **"All right, then, have it your way.**
>
> —CS LEWIS

God wants you to take what He has given you and make deposits into the lives of other people. When you make a deposit into someone else, God's investment has begun to grow and multiply. God's investment has begun to increase. Then God wants that person, in turn, to make a deposit of his own into someone else. The world's first and finest network marketing plan! The most successful, too! And the whole network is built on the two-way street of trust. I trust God, and God trusts me.

Isn't it amazing how Christians are always talking about trusting God, as if trust is a one-way street? Isn't it amazing how, when you talk about trust, it's usually something like, "I'm trusting you, God." And all the time, God is asking: "Have I ever failed you? Can you point to history and show Me where I ever failed anyone?"

"No, God, I can't say that You've ever failed anybody."

"Then, isn't that a pretty good basis for you to trust Me?"

"Oh, yes, God. I really trust you."

"Okay, now, what about My being able to trust you? I've made a deposit in you. Do I not have the right to expect a return? If I give you My salvation, if I give you My healing, if I give you My deliverance, do I not have a right to expect a return from My deposit . . . My investment in your life?"

"But how can I give you a return on your investment, Lord?"

"You can give Me a return by living a life that is exemplary. You can give Me a return by letting your light shine before a watching world. You can give Me a return by being faithful with the truths I've deposited inside of you and by faithfully depositing those same things in others. You can give Me a return by the sparkle of your Diamond Life living as a model husband, model wife, model employee, and model citizen. You can give Me a return by not being depressed, oppressed, cast down, and overwhelmed by the weight of the world. Shine, sparkle, dazzle with the brilliance of My wisdom and knowledge working through every facet of your living."

Every relationship is based upon mutual, two-way trust. If you bank, for example, your relationship with the bank is a two-way relationship of trust. You trust the bank with your money. You trust that your money will be safeguarded, that proper interest will be paid to you for use of your money, and that an accurate accounting of your disbursements will be maintained. But your bank also trusts you.

"How?" you might ask.

For one thing the bank trusts that you won't write checks totaling more than you have deposited.

And trust is foundational in any personal or professional relationship. For a relationship to survive, both parties must be able to trust one another with confidential information they deposit into each other. If that trust is violated even once, it could irreparably damage the relationship. And if the violation of trust is repetitive, the relationship will terminate.

Jesus said, "If you want to be trusted with greater things, you must prove trustworthy with that which another man has surrendered to your care."

People wonder sometimes why they don't see more of God's abundance in their lives. "Why did she get the promotion instead of me?" they ask. "Why does she make more money? Why did she get a raise, while I didn't? Why does she have the job and I don't?"

Is it possible you can't be trusted with what belongs to another? If you cheat on your job in terms of time or production, you are being unfaithful to the man who is managing your work. If you fail to exercise the gifts God has deposited within you, you are being unfaithful to the God who saved you and invested in you. Trust is important. When God talks about something 134 times in the Bible, I can assure you it is important.

The apostle Paul wrote, "Moreover it is required in stewards that one be found faithful" (I Corinthians 4:2). If you've been entrusted with something of value, then it behooves you to prove yourself faithful. In fact, it is required by God that you prove yourself faithful.

God expressed confidence in you when He deposited an inheritance into your trust account long before you were saved, believing that you would respond to His plan for your life as a trustworthy administrator of that deposit. And He trusts you still, by counting on you to be an integral part of His plan for meeting the needs of the world.

If you fail in your responsibility of trust, God's plan for you and the world suffers. But as you faithfully respond and others respond to God's trust His plan has a chance to function efficiently in your life and in the earth. Trust is truly the foundation of The Diamond Life. The Diamond Life offers you the greatest opportunity to live securely without fear.

In as much as a diamond is often used as a gift to someone, in the same sense, your Diamond Life is a gift from God to you and from you to others, the world, and to His Kingdom. In this sense, its greatest value is when it's deposited.

LIFE GEMS

From Chapter Eight

We love because we need.
God needs because He loves.

Trust is one of the most neglected principles of life.

Everything God created gives and makes deposits into human lives.

Trust means to be secure without fear.

You were intended for the purposes of the Kingdom of God.

His desire for you is significance.

All that you possess is a trust deposit from God.

CHAPTER NINE

"Your" Trust Deposit

Sharing the Wealth

> **A life becomes great by the investing of it to make the world a better place.**

You are rich beyond your wildest imagination! Literally everything you need for life is now on deposit with your name on the account. And the account is set up to increase dramatically with use. You and I have an inheritance of a Diamond Life promised to us by God. He makes a deposit of trust into our account, in order to complete and perfect us in our purpose. It is the most valuable gift that you and I ever receive. It is the way God reveals Himself to the world. The more you use it, make withdrawals, and then deposit into others' lives, the more you will have for yourself.

In the previous chapter, you were introduced to the biblical word *trust* as a verb. But "trust" is also a noun. Something (some thing) is actually committed to your keeping and care by God. The something that has been committed to my care and to yours is the sum total of all the treasures, all the knowledge, and the gifts, and all the talents of life. God has given you these things as a deposit in your earthly accounts, from which you draw to fulfill your purposes in the world. The deposits do you no good if left in the bank. They must be drawn upon and invested in your Kingdom purpose.

We must always remember that God's things are entrusted to you for safe keeping and for wise use. You are not the owner of these things; you are the trustee. You are the manager of the truths and the blessings that God gives. If these things are to be utilized in a manner that will glorify God, then they must be used to draw, win, and nurture people. They must be used to accomplish God's purpose in the world through the various individuals that comprise it.

The Transfer of Deposits

God does not bring people into my life by accident. When people enter my sphere of influence, however briefly, they enter it because He has determined they need to cross the path of my life. He knows certain individuals who need the things I have, and He knows certain other individuals who possess the things I need. These "things" may be tangible. But they may also be experiences, wisdom, insights, information, concern, encouragement, or even a simple smile or pat on the back.

How do you greet someone who crosses your path? Do

you ask his or her name? Do you introduce yourself and take the time to learn the person's name? You should! A simple gesture like a kind word provides you with an opportunity to deposit something into the life of another human being. Remember, when someone crosses your path, it's usually because he or she is looking for someone to deposit something of benefit into his or her life.

A diamond becomes a diamond because of what the earth deposits into it. The value of that diamond, however, can never be revealed as long as it is hidden in the earth. The discovery of that diamond only happens when someone goes out of their way to dig it up. God says: "Listen! I have loved you and I have deposited My truth within you. Shouldn't you be reaching out to others with the same love?" Yet your flesh drives you to familiar turf. When you attend functions and go about your normal routines, you tend to migrate toward your comfort zones, your surface level kind of living. You tend to huddle with your familiar crowds. You're likely to safeguard your privacy behind security fences, smoked windshields, and mirrored sunglasses.

In a sense, I am God's "bank" and I must remember that fact. He has deposited certain entities within me, and He desires to find those things at His disposal whenever and wherever He wishes to use them to accomplish His purposes. He is the owner of the salvation experience within me, and I am the guardian. He expects to use my life as a living example of His transforming power as the world watches me live. He is the owner of the gospel within me, and I am the guardian. He is the owner of the peace within me, the love, the joy. I am the guardian, and I must make God's resources available to Him or He will withdraw His resources and deposit them elsewhere.

Counsel in the heart of man is like water in a deep well, but a man of understanding draws it out. (Proverbs 20:5, AMP)

Trust Defined

What is a trust?

Black's Law Dictionary says that a trust is "a right of property, real or personal, held by one party for the benefit of another; any arrangement whereby property is transferred with the intention that it be administered by a trustee for another's benefit."

A trust, therefore, is a process, a legal arrangement, an agreement by which property is transferred to someone else with the intention that the person who receives the trust is able to use it for the benefit of the person who gave the trust or for others involved in it.

1 Chronicles 29:14 (GNT) states, "Everything is a gift from you, and we have only given back what is yours already." What a powerful verse of Scripture! You give back to God only what originally came from Him in the first place. Your very life came from God.

In 1 Corinthians 4:7, Paul asks, "What do you have that you did not receive?" What do you own? What do you possess that the Lord has not given to you? The answer is quite obvious. I own nothing. I have nothing except that which God has given me. "Naked I came from my mother's womb, naked I'll return to the womb of the earth. God gives, God takes. God's name be ever blessed" (Job 1:21 MSG).

So, do you think God gave life and all its benefits to me for my own personal possession? Did God give it to me to hoard? Did God give it to me to save? Did God give it to me just to hide away? No! The Master would say, "You ought to have deposited my money with the bankers, and at my coming I would have received back my own with interest" (Matthew 25:27). It's as if Jesus is saying: "Go into the marketplace and do business for me, because I am giving you a trust. I am entrusting to you some money, some possessions. I am investing in you, and when I come back I'm going to require of you what you've done with the trust that I've given you. I am investing in you The Diamond Life, strategically placed in a setting where I receive the most glory. Someday, I will require of you an accounting, for the deposit of trust of The Diamond Life." You, my friend, are Christ's investment.

But remember this: trust is a two-way street. The Diamond Life is not just about your trust in God; it's also about God's trust in you. God has made an everlasting deposit into your life. He has established a "legal" trust between you and the Kingdom of Heaven. And God trusts you to do something about that covenant commitment. He is expecting you to live up to your end of the agreement, to give back to Him with interest those things He has given to you.

Life-Enhancing Deposits (L.E.D)

God is a generous God. He has enriched your life, as He has enriched mine. He has enhanced your life faithfully and abundantly.

He is a generous and unfailing God. He masterfully crafted your Diamond Life as He interacted with you in your daily challenges. When you didn't see value in your circumstance, He actually was working out a great promise of reward. You didn't always look like a diamond and when a diamond is discovered it doesn't either.

Mentally and emotionally, He has blessed you with:

Purpose
Direction
Self-worth
Happiness
Destiny

Physically, He has blessed you with:

Strength
Health
Wealth
Relationships
Employment

Spiritually, He has blessed you with:

Salvation
Peace
Joy
Anointing
Divine revelation

If you really want to understand the faithfulness and generosity of God, simply look at His creation. He is truly trustworthy, because, as He promised, "While the earth remains, seedtime and harvest, and cold and heat, and winter and summer, and day and night shall not cease" (Genesis 8:22). He is truly generous, because everything He has made produces in overabundance. I am told, for example, that most bananas fall to the ground and rot. Less than half the bananas in the world are consumed by man and beast, because banana trees produce more than harvesters can pick and process. The same is true of other fruits and vegetables, as well. God is a generous God.

But I have to remember that, when God gives to me faithfully and generously, He is also making a demand on my life. He is saying, "When you get this deposit of trust, I expect . . ." No, actually He goes farther than that! He says, "I *demand* . . . that you share what I've given to you with someone else, that you give out as I have given to you." The duty of the trustee is to use the trust for the benefit of the custodian. And that, in a nutshell, is what

God expects from you and from me. The beauty, value, and benefit of a diamond is best seen after the deposits of the earth are complete and the craftsman makes his deposits to craft it.

Is there any wonder that some Christians are bankrupt? Is there any wonder that some Christians are sick, weak, anemic, struggling, and gasping for breath spiritually? No joy! No peace! No power! No victory! Is it any wonder that many believers are depressed, oppressed, and lonely? That they feel angry at God because of something that has happened in their lives? And all the time, God is saying: "Listen, friend. You are the trustee of a trust. When I gave you that trust, I expected you to do what I did. I gave it away to you, and I expected you to give it away to somebody else. You are struggling in many areas of your life, because, like the servant with the one talent, you have buried my trust in the ground. You have not used it for my glory and its value is not being seen in your life. A diamond never seen has very little use and purpose."

What did Jesus say? He said, "If you give as little as a drink of cold water in my name, you have given it to Me." But what is "a drink of cold water"? A drink of cold water can save the life of someone who is lost in a desert. Water is refreshment. Water is life. And when you give "a drink of cold water," it might be given in the form of refreshment for the soul of one who is struggling through a dry place in life.

When you show warmth, when you are friendly, when

you shake someone's hand and greet him or her with a smile, when you ask someone's name...the smallest things can make a real difference in a person's life. For that reason, the best place to begin making deposits is in your own family and among your own circle of friends. People in your family need your acceptance, affirmation, and affection. Your friends need your encouragement, support, and assistance. On the Day of Accounting, when you stand before God, an explanation will be needed of how you responded to the people in need that He sent into your life.

All trusts have stipulations. When a wealthy man establishes a trust fund for one of his children, he might dictate a maximum amount of funds that can be withdrawn each year for personal use by the child. The same is true of God's trust. God has entrusted you with great things, but He is the One who tells you what to do and how to do it. He is the One who commands you to minister to the "least of these." A child may not like all the stipulations of the trust that his father establishes for him, but he would be a fool to decline the trust. We, too, would be foolish indeed to reject our heavenly Father's trust.

But if you accept the trust that your heavenly Father has given you, then you must follow the dictates of the trust. You must be willing to deposit God's wealth into "the least" of God's people. You must be willing to do "the least" of all ministries. Despite the fact that many are lured to the more visible areas of Christian service (music, teaching, leadership), you must all be willing to do what is unseen, what is unheralded, and what is seemingly unappreciated by others.

I know someone who has a living trust that was established for him in the 1940s. Each year, he withdraws a certain amount of money, but the compound interest continues to strengthen the fund from year to year. On one occasion, I asked this man how much money was contained in the fund.

"I don't know," he said.

"You mean that you don't know exactly," I said. "But I'm not interested in the exact figure. I just want to know about how much you have in the fund."

"I have no idea," he replied.

"You mean, you don't have any concept of how much money you have?" I inquired.

"That's right!" he exclaimed.

"Don't you want to know?" I asked.

"Well, I guess so," he said.

But he didn't know even the approximate balance of the trust fund, and he had no real plans to find out.

The same is true for many people. You have no concept of the things that God has entrusted to your care. You have no idea what the balance is in your spiritual accounts, your Kingdom worth—the value of your Diamond Life. But you need to know. You need to take occasional inventory of your lives. Because the Master has made a deposit into your life and because He continues to make deposits on regular occasions, you must know what He has deposited within you and what He wants you to do with it. And even though the Master has gone away on a journey, He will eventually return and call you to give an account to Him for every deposit He made into you.

There was once a gentleman who wandered into our church on a Sunday morning. The man lived in Nova Scotia, but he was traveling through Ohio, so he randomly decided to visit our Sunday services. This man was so touched by the ministry of the Word, he purchased a CD copy of the message following the service that morning.

During his flight home, later that day, this man listened to the message again. He was moved to tears, because the message really touched a need in his life. When he got home, he called his wife to his side, and together they listened to the audio, worshipping and weeping all the while. Then, the man called together several of his friends from his local church. On a particular evening in his home, this group of people sat in the man's house, listening to this tape.

Not long ago, I received a letter from this man. In the letter, he told me how my message on that particular Sunday morning had caused a great breakthrough for the people in his local church in Nova Scotia. He also told me that people were continuing to listen to the tape. Lives were being changed. Good things were happening.

I have thought a lot about that letter. What a marvelous illustration of how God can take your faithful use of His deposits within you and make a deposit into another man's life. And isn't it amazing how that deposit can be spread from person to person to person? I deposited my ability to teach (God's deposit in me) into that man. He deposited it into his wife. They deposited it into the hearts of a few friends. And they deposited it into an entire church. Thus you see the process of The Diamond Life producing residual effects far beyond imagination.

God is ready to make incredible deposits into your life, which will cause you to shine with the brilliance of a diamond.

The saying goes that "A diamond is forever." I would say The Diamond Life He has chosen for us to live produces forever effects. The purpose of your deposit trust, The Diamond Life, is to reveal the beauty and splendor of His life though you. His desire is for your true beauty to be seen and personified by the world as you share the wealth of His deposits.

From Chapter Nine

You are the manager of the truths
and the blessings that God gives.

You are Christ's investment.

God's purpose is you becoming a diamond.

God makes regular deposits into your life.

Your Diamond Life produces
forever effects.

CHAPTER TEN

"Your" Beauty Within

Inner Beauty Discovered

Jesus came to reveal man to himself just as much as He came to reveal God to man.

Even a diamond that is not mounted is a thing of beauty. Lying against the background of black velvet, it scintillates in brilliance. But mounted in a gold, silver, or platinum setting—a delicate silver necklace of intricate design, an old-fashioned filigree gold ring, a simple bezel earring motif, a platinum domed band with champagne diamonds, an ornate pave bracelet—it exceeds beauty and rises to splendor and magnificence.

The setting, or mounting, makes the difference. It draws out all the glory of the diamond for the world to view. In like manner, The Diamond Life permits the world to witness the beauty and excellence of a life committed to Christ. It begins within. Your beauty within is discovered the moment you trust Him with your life.

Trust: a two-way street

All Christians should trust God. In fact, "without faith it is impossible to please Him" (Hebrews 11:6). But faith is a two-way street. So if I intend to be effective in the world as a Christian, then I must come to the place in life where God can trust me as well. The beauty He placed within me will only be revealed as I place my complete and full trust in Him.

It's interesting that the Bible has a great deal to say about people's need to trust God, but very little to say about God trusting them. I often wondered about that until I realized the reason for the overemphasis on one side of the street and the near neglect on the other. You see, God often repeats principles and mandates in Scripture, because He knows His people need to be constantly reminded of their part in a covenant. Unless God regularly calls His people back to the principles of the covenants He has made with them, they will wander away from those principles and forget their responsibilities.

But God never forgets His part in a covenant. If He has said something just once in the written Word, it shall be accomplished exactly as He said it. God doesn't need, therefore, to remind human beings of His trust in them. But He needs to constantly remind them to trust in Him.

And there is an interesting cycle here. When you trust God, you step into a dimension of Christian living that makes it possible for God to trust you. And as God trusts you and you see the results of that trust, you, in turn, trust

Him more. The relationship grows and grows, producing boldness, power, and fruit. But that kind of relationship cycle begins when you step out and trust God.

"For he who comes to God must believe that He is, and that He is a rewarder of those who diligently seek Him" (Hebrews 11:6). The two-way street of faith and trust begins with you and me, not with God, because God has already given us the faith to believe.

> **I know God will not give me anything I can't handle. I just wish that He didn't trust me so much.**
>
> —MOTHER TERESA

How can you know if you have the kind of trust that will cause God to trust you? Simple! Note how your trust (faith) sustains you during difficult times. Anyone can trust God when everything is going right. Anybody can trust God when there are no problems. But do you trust God when all hell breaks loose? Do you trust Him when your prayers seemingly go unanswered? Do you trust Him when it seems as if He has abandoned you?

People usually don't walk away from God when everything is going great. However, very often people walk away from God when the chips are down.

Many years ago, one of my mentors, G.W. Lane, instructed me, "You should never make major decisions during down times." In other words, he was telling me that

I should never make a decision to take a step backward when circumstances are negative. I shouldn't resign a position when passing through difficulties. I should never resign when I am discouraged.

Resignations should always be made on the mountaintop, where everything is wonderful, after all your prayers have been answered, when faith abounds in your heart. When you take a step backward while things are wonderful, you can rest assured that the Spirit of God motivates that move.

I salute the wisdom of my mentor. I believe God gave him a powerful principle to share with me. No person should ever quit, when life is at its worst. When the person stands at a difficult crossroads, he or she should find the positives in the situation, renew resolve, draw closer to God, and ride out the storm in confidence. One should never quit in a time of adversity. Of course, there are exceptions to all rules.

Everything that Christians are and everything they possess constitutes a sacred trust from God.

Their souls, their bodies, their time, their possessions—everything is a gift from God. In addition, God puts a trust within them–His message. The message does not depend on individuals for its credibility or authority. I don't have to give credibility to the message of Jesus Christ. I never have to give it authority. I am a fool if I even attempt to explain it or defend it; if I try to make it work or make it happen. I am not responsible to heal, save, or deliver people. I am merely the messenger, the depositor. The message is able to take care of itself.

Adorned with Beauty

The Diamond Life is truly a deposit. It will become a living spiritual force within. It will manifest itself through your mouth, through your eyes, through your thoughts. It will gain life through your actions and behaviors, your attitudes and your actions. It will be demonstrated through your habits, your language, your disposition, your work ethic, your morals, and your interaction with other people. And The Diamond Life becomes attractive by the way you live it. It is designed to make you a magnet, drawing people into the Kingdom through you, your witness, and your testimony. (We will discuss more about this in the next chapter.) The deposit of The Diamond Life is designed to make you an adornment of God. The most basic use of diamonds is for adornment; but there is outward adorning and there is inward adorning. Your beauty within is never more important than when you face life's challenges. Sometimes life tries to "ugly your life." In those moments, your inner beauty will sustain you. People see your beauty within and are drawn to the message of Christ.

God wants you to know that The Diamond Life is deposited within you to adorn you on the inside. The Diamond Life will affect your demeanor and change your mind.

It will rearrange your priorities and alter your path; it will make you a person of beauty, honor, and power. When it is deposited within you and manifested through God's trust in you, people will seek you out, regardless of your status in life. You will be a person of inner beauty and attraction, because you will be able to give a reason for the hope that is within you to everyone who asks. You will become attractive to God, attractive to yourself and your family, and attractive to those around you, drawing them to The Diamond Life.

> *He has made everything beautiful in its time. He also has planted eternity in men's hearts and minds [a divinely implanted sense of a purpose working through the ages which nothing under the sun but God alone can satisfy], yet so that men cannot find out what God has done from the beginning to the end (Ecclesiastes 3:11, AMP).*

God has made all of His people beautiful within, and He has given them the same Diamond Life deposit. And because that deposit comes out through your inner personal beauty, it is exhibited in different ways through different people. However, the life is the same, the power is the same, the attraction is the same, and the appeal is the same. When the deposit of God—Kingdom laws and principles—finds its way out of you through your countenance, your words, your actions, and your attitudes, you may rest assured that people will be drawn to you and to Christ through you.

How do you come to that place in your life, the place where the adornment of the Kingdom laws and principles, shines through your unique inner beauty and positively impacts your life? People will take note of the fact that there is something different about you; they will desire that thing; and they will approach you, asking you to tell them what is different in your life.

Then, share your life. When you do, God always makes a compensating deposit into your trust account. When you give to somebody, God gives to you. You can't out-give God. It's that simple! If you want more of what God has to give, then all you have to do is give away what He has already given to you. Deposit it into someone else who needs it, and then tell them to do likewise.

We become God's adornment, masterfully crafted, designed by Him, from within, to draw people into His Kingdom. Our inner beauty is then defined by the life that is revealed through the challenges we face day-by-day.

When you make a deposit into someone else's life, God makes a deposit into yours.

Remember, it's the pressing, the crushing, and the polishing that brings out the beauty of the diamond. Your inner beauty is best revealed as you endure the process and conquer the challenges of your life.

LIFE GEMS

From Chapter Ten

Never quit during a down time.

Trust God always, regardless.

Your Diamond Life becomes attractive by the way you live it.

"Your" Destiny

Your Treasure M.A.P.

I know what I'm doing. I have it all planned out—plans to take care of you, not abandon you, plans to give you the future you hope for.
(Jeremiah 29:11, MSG)

For we are God's [own] handiwork (His workmanship), recreated in Christ Jesus, [born anew] that we may do those good works which God predestined (planned beforehand) for us [taking paths which He prepared ahead of time], that we should walk in them [living the good life which He prearranged and made ready for us to live].
(Ephesians 2:10, AMP)

At any given time, your life may not be the beautiful, rewarding, confident, fearless one you desire to live. Your location is only important as it relates to your destination. God can always take you from where you are (regardless of where you are) to where He desires you to be.

There is always more positive within you than the negative that surrounds you. In photography, you expose a negative to controlled light to produce a picture. God shines His light of revelation, wisdom, and knowledge into our hearts where we have allowed negative thoughts to deceive us. The Diamond Life brings out the best, the treasure, the beauty, the authenticity of the real you. You must be convinced always that His ultimate goal is His purpose fulfilled through you. Whatever heat, pressure, and time He must permit into your life for your Diamond Life to be revealed, you can be confident in His decisions.

The M.A.P. (Master-Assigned Path) guarantees that He already has chosen your route and designed your life to discover your treasure. That means you will have to pursue His path and be determined to arrive at your destination, your God-assigned destination.

CHAPTER ELEVEN

"Your" Beauty Experienced

Attraction Guaranteed

When you live His life, your inward beauty will captivate the world around you.

Diamonds sparkle and glisten with beauty and give a message of genuineness and authenticity. It is the beauty of the diamond, in its setting, that is always the object of attention. Therefore, it is with each of us.

When God places His life in you, He does so with a particular purpose in mind. God does not do things merely so you and I can enjoy them; He has a greater purpose. When God places His deposit of life into you, He places it there so it can be shared with others. And His desire is for you to pass His deposit along to others, who in turn will pass it along to others.

The Diamond Life creates a belief system by which I live my life. No longer do I operate by the belief systems of the world. No longer do I operate by my own standards and practices of a world that has lost its way. No longer do I operate by the moral compass and practices of a world that is earmarked for death and decay. Instead, when the deposit of God gets into my life, I am filled with a new attitude and a new purpose for life that propels me down a pathway of Christ-likeness and greatness. This deposit of God makes me attractive to the world.

Let this trust deposit of life remind you that you have to protect and safeguard what God has put inside you. It is an incredible trust, a trust of the most treasured truth the world has even known: the message of Jesus Christ. When you come to the place as a Diamond Life-seeker that you become the message (preach what you practice), then you must jealously protect the sacred trust that you have gained.

What matters is not your outer appearance—
the styling of your hair, the jewelry you wear, the
cut of your clothes—but your inner disposition.
(1 Peter 3:4, MSG)

When Peter speaks about the "beauty" of the hidden man of the heart, he is describing someone who is gentle, tender, humble, mild, and considerate. He is writing about a spirit that is disciplined and under control at all times. This spirit does not flare up, talk back, act defensively, cut in, rant, rave, or go on talking and talking. It does not whine or whimper or appear persecuted or take on a martyr complex. And that's what God wants you to be like. He wants you to adorn yourself with The Diamond Life and get rid of whimpering and defensive attitudes. He wants to rid you of the victim complex. In this way, you begin to define the beauty of your Diamond Life. In each season of your life (more about this in Chapter 12), He is looking for the consistency of the true value, like that contained in a true, certified diamond. Regardless of where you find it—lying in the mud, lost in a pond—the value never changes. Whatever has happened to you should never diminish the value of your life. Regardless of any sin you've committed, He forgives, transforms, renews, and restores the true beauty of your life as you enjoy His forgiveness. Nothing that ever happens to you or within you decreases your worth. In His eyes, you are always a diamond in the rough, always in the process of developing your true value and true beauty.

You may not always look like a diamond as you live your life, but that doesn't mean you aren't.

Following His M.A.P.

God is always more concerned about your destination than He is about your location. Regardless of your current location (trials, challenges, circumstances, adversities, obstacles, failures), God always looks at your destiny (destination). Location does not hinder destination. Your true beauty is revealed as you live your God-assignment. He redeems your detours.

As you work through the process and prove yourself faithful in the world, you get increasing opportunities. The value of your inner person creates new opportunities in your life. Life challenges out of you the treasure that is buried within you. The black piece of coal hides the beauty of the diamond until it is freed from the dirt and debris that surrounds it. He is always trying to reveal to the world around us the great treasure He put within us. The exact same thing is true in the Kingdom of God, because whatever happens in the world is a mere copy of what happens in the Kingdom. The Law of Increasing Opportunity works in both the physical domain and the spiritual domain. God beautifies the meek with salvation for the purpose of increasing our influence to the world.

Whatever your circumstance, bloom where you are planted. Begin to live The Diamond Life where you are, with the faith that you now have. Begin to use the grace that has already been given to you. As you exercise what you already have—even if your faith is only the size of a mustard seed—you will begin to grow in grace and faith. And as you grow by using what has already been entrusted to you, you will learn to trust God more and more. Then God will trust you more and more. In and through every season of your life, maintain your trust in the process of creating your Diamond Life. Your faith and faithfulness will demonstrate to all onlookers that you are committed to the Lord for the long haul. Doors will open to you in ever-increasing measure, as God is able to trust you with more. Thus, this cycle of spiritual growth and opportunity continues throughout your earthly life. Living The Diamond Life increases your value, not only in the world around you, but in His Kingdom as well. You are measuring your treasure.

Regardless of your season, your value does not change.

Matthew 25:29 really summarizes this premise best: "For to everyone who has, more will be given, and he will have abundance; but from him who does not have, even what he has will be taken away." The man or woman who has will get more. To him shall be given great abundance. This is the Law of Increasing Opportunity. And how do I qualify for this blessing? Through faithfulness! Simple faithfulness! The most important component for capturing God's attention and moving His hand is faithfulness. But trust takes time to develop. Nothing will ever dominate your life unless you do it daily. Be consistent. No person will trust me beyond the point that I have proven myself to be worthy of trust. It takes time to build trust, and that trust is built by manifesting faithfulness day after day, week after week, month after month, year after year. The proof of desire is pursuit. I am talking about the seasons of your life as you are living The Diamond Life where trust and true beauty are defined.

Love Amplified

When a man gives a diamond ring to his wife, he may get her attention, but it won't establish her trust. It may not even increase love, but when a husband loves his wife by his continuing faithfulness, that love is amplified. It is multiplied and spread. When a husband loves his wife, that love is diffused. It is distributed to others in greater measure than it was received. When a husband loves his wife in the way Christ loved the church, the wife turns around and loves her children, loves her father-in-law, loves her mother-in-law, loves her sister, her brother, her nephews, aunts, and cousins. She loves her neighbors and even loves disagreeable people. She also loves her husband with more intensity than ever. She's an amplifier, a diffuser of the love of God. However, God wants that love to be sown into her by her husband. He also wants spiritual truth to be sown into her by her husband. A woman is never more beautiful than when her husband is faithful to God, to her, and to his family.

Every woman is connected with a man in some way. Whether it is a husband, a father, a pastor, or a spiritual friend—every woman is spiritually connected with a male mentor. And I can always tell when that woman is being loved in the way God intended for her to be loved. The woman who is properly and appropriately loved by her male mentor is a woman who is not depressed. She is not oppressed. She's not beaten down. She has self-esteem and self-worth. Everywhere this woman goes, the love of God flows from her because she is an amplifier and a diffuser of the love that has been placed within her. There's a gleam in her eye. There's a smile on her face. She cannot do enough for her family or for others. Love creates beauty, inwardly and outwardly. The strength of a marriage may not be enhanced by the giving of a diamond, but a Diamond Life of commitment, devotion, and love will cause the marriage to be strong, enduring. That woman is never more beautiful than when she experiences God's love for her and through her.

Ephesians 2:10 says that you are His workmanship. The word workmanship comes from a root word meaning "poem." You are God's workmanship. You are God's poem. This means the Divine Poet is writing a poem full of the rhyme and the rhythm of Heaven, and you are the theme of that poem. You are His artistic product. He is writing a poem about your life that will be read by all. Your life, your beauty, your effectiveness is defined by His poem. Knowing He has written this poem about your life enables you to walk along the path He has specifically mandated for you.

Finding Your Treasure on His M.A.P.

There's nothing more poetic than living The Diamond Life. Like any poem, some of the lines may be difficult to understand, especially when they are taken out of the context of the poem as a whole. If you analyze any single line of a poem, it may not make sense. You have to read the poem in its entirety, interpreting each line in the context of the entire work. The same is true with your life. The individual occurrences in your life will make little sense if you isolate them from the other occurrences. We must see all the experiences of life—good and bad—as part of God's overall plan that will lead to a final, beautiful masterpiece. God does not see you as a bunch of pieces, events, acts, but as a whole. He never perfects us one piece at a time–but is concerned with wholeness. God has designed your life to be revealed through everything you experience. A diamond is not created; it is discovered as you live life.

All people are born with a calling on their lives that is meant to be carried out through the expressions of gifts, talents, and abilities. Life can be lived to the fullest measure only when people abandon themselves to the master passion God has put within (The Diamond Life).

In reality, everything you face in life, God uses to unveil and reveal the beauty and value of your Diamond Life.

Once you discover and define your calling, you can then organize your life around it. Everything you do should be an expression of your calling. Without a calling to guide you, your goals and action plans may not ultimately fulfill you. Identifying, acknowledging, and living your calling is the most important action you can take. Your calling must be discovered, embraced, and lived with passion and enthusiasm. Those who fail to do this get sidetracked on life's journey. It's easy to wander and drift, accomplishing little.

When you are truly living your calling, the people, resources, and opportunities you need will supernaturally gravitate toward you. In God's Word, it's called a Law of Attraction; He purposefully created you to be attractive, and living The Diamond Life magnifies that attraction. That is why a completely unknown person can suddenly be put front and center on life's stage as they live their purpose. It is the diamond inside the coal that causes people to mine the coal. The attraction of the coal is the diamond. Your attraction is living The Diamond Life. His favor within you means you are targeted, marked for blessing, favor which makes you attractive to others.

The world benefits, too, because when you are in alignment with your calling your actions will serve others. God does not change His mind about your calling and gifting. He never withdraws them once they are given, and He does not change His mind about those to whom He gives His grace or to whom He sends His call.

- ♦ God is the originator of all things – all things come from Him.
- ♦ God originated your calling and gifting–He chose them for you.
- ♦ God is the sustainer of all things–they all depend on Him.
- ♦ God sustains your calling and gifting–No one can change your calling and gifting or stop them.

Romans 11:36 is one of the greatest of all statements about God.

- ♦ "For of Him" – A reminder that He is the source of all things.
- ♦ "And through Him" – A reminder that He is the sustainer of all things.
- ♦ "And to Him" – A reminder that He is the significance of all things.

God created you so that He could call you and gift you to perpetuate His Kingdom on earth. His calling and His gifts through your Diamond Life are a part of the beauty of your salvation.

As the One from whom you come, you know Him as source. As the One who keeps you alive in every dimension, you recognize Him as the force. And because it is to Him that you are continually moving, you gladly acknowledge Him as the course of your life.

Remember this as you continue to journey into your Diamond Life…

According to Ephesians 2:10, each person has a divine assignment—"that we may do those good works which God predestined for us." Each person has a divine path—a road with your name on it—("taking paths which He prepared ahead of time") that we should walk in them ("living the good life which He prearranged and made ready for you to live"). The tools He has given you—gifts, talents, abilities, influence, and position—work best within your assignments. A hammer won't cut and a saw will not drive nails. You are perfectly built, and placed in His Kingdom to be significantly successful.

When you come to Jesus Christ, if indeed you have, you come as a diamond in the rough. You come with faults, flaws, and imperfections. You come with hidden beauty, but nobody, including yourself, is able to see that beauty. But Jesus saw beauty, potential, and worth in you when nobody else did. Consequently, He paid a high price to purchase you and He will spend a lifetime perfecting you.

As a diamond, you were formed by heat. And as a diamond, you are a potential masterpiece in the artist's hand. He will cut you where you need to be cut. He will polish you as you need to be polished. He will shine you up and place you in an exalted setting (strategic position), where the world can see His workmanship in you.

> **Diamonds are only chunks of coal**
> **that stuck to their jobs, you see.**
>
> —MINNIE RICHARD SMITH

You, my friend, are His delight, the apple of His eye. He has invested much in you, because He believes in you. You, in turn, now must invest your all in Him.

In every season of your life, maintain your faithfulness and trust in Him. He will cause your Diamond Life to shine through no matter what season you are in.

LIFE GEMS

From Chapter Eleven

The deposit of God makes you attractive to the world.

Nothing that ever happens to you or within you decreases your worth.

God is always more concerned about your destination than He is about your location.

Always bloom where you are planted.

Nothing will ever dominate your life unless you do it daily. You are God's poem.

Everything you do should be an expression of your calling.

CHAPTER TWELVE

The Value of "Your" Seasons

Embrace Your Seasons

> **Winter is an etching, spring a watercolor,**
> **summer an oil painting and autumn**
> **a mosaic of them all.**
>
> -STANLEY HOROWITZ

No diamond is ever formed without millions of years of heat and pressure. The Diamond Life is never complete without the experience of many seasons. Every season of The Diamond Life will produce value. Someone has said, "Everything gets better with age."

Life for each of us is mirrored in the four physical seasons of the earth: winter, spring, summer and fall.

As people grow and mature, they must understand the need to embrace their changing seasons. They must grasp the necessity to not miss a single season of life. Every season is important. Every season has value.

The seasons are basically divided into four types:

The Season of Seedtime –
You are sowing seeds. You are getting prepared.

The Season of Growth –
You experience development.

The Season of Harvest –
You reap what you have sown during seedtime.

The Season of Renewal –
You rest and rejuvenate.

And so throughout life, you have four types of seasons on an ongoing, continuous basis.

I need to know what season I am in. I need to see the season for what it is. I need to know what I am supposed to learn and perform in that season.

- ♦ How shall I live in this moment of my season?
- ♦ Shall I live with faith or shall I be saddled with doubt?
- ♦ Shall I have life and energy or shall I be oppressed and depressed?

When we cooperate with the season, God then begins to line up things, people, and resources to assist us in that season.

Every season is a P.E.T.—a Personal Empowerment Time. It is in the moment when you don't like a season that it is most likely going to empower you. Every season is also a P.D.T.—Personal Discipleship Time. Whatever the season, God helps you maneuver through it. He gives grace, but not necessarily in advance; grace is activated at the point of need. There is no pre-grace. He will give you a vision, but not until He is ready for you to move into it.

How you respond to a season depends upon your understanding of your season and your level of maturity.

Enduring the Wait

Every season has a time of beauty. You have inside of you a sense of eternity, a sense of divine purpose, and the only way you will ever understand your life is to understand the purpose for which God created you. You cannot understand your life outside of God's purpose. You must wait until you get to the end of the season to see what God is going to do with it. Look for a moment at a tree in winter; how ugly and lifeless it appears. Soon that tree will develop and grow into the promise of spring. It will come to the fullness of summer, and it will eventually arrive at a fall harvest when the fruit is ripe for harvesting. I don't have to look at my current season as permanent; it will come to an end.

Every season has an appointed purpose in producing destiny. Henry David Thoreau, the philosopher, wrote this:

> **Live in each season as it passes, breathe the air, drink the drink, taste the fruit and resign yourself to the influences of whatever is going on. Let them be your only diet, only drink, and botanical medicines.**
>
> —HENRY DAVID THOREAU

Some do that with seasons. They take out the nutritional value of the season by taking out what they don't like. But you must embrace the unpleasantness of your season, because what's unpleasant to you is not necessarily unpleasant to God. When Jesus Christ died on the Cross, it was ugly to humanity. It was ugly to Jesus himself. Yet, He endured it and embraced it fully. He said, "I am willing to drink the cup of death and die that I might bring salvation to mankind." Perhaps we should remember this was 4,000 years in the making from Genesis to the end of the Old Testament. There were many seasons in the Kingdom of God for the life of man. All of those seasons were necessary for God to perfect the process of His salvation. So the New Testament says, "In the fullness of times, God sent forth His son Jesus." "Fullness of times" means everything was made ready for His arrival. That is a theological lesson that we don't need to get into here, but the point is it took time, seasons to develop, to prepare, to make ready the entrance of God into the earth. Perhaps men would've avoided some of those seasons to help speed up the process, but not God. If the diamond is extracted from the coal before the heat, pressure, and time process, it is not fully formed, not matured, not complete. The value of the product is greatly diminished.

We see this in nature when fruit is pulled before its time, before it's mature. The taste, quality, goodness, and nutrition must be given time to produce the desired, valuable product. Heat, pressure, and time are all necessary to The Diamond Life process.

Perhaps it is the time part that's the most difficult for us. We always want to speed up the process and get to the reward. Always keep in mind, He knows best and The Diamond Life is a process.

The Reason for Your Seasons

Seasons develop and mature you. God's greatest priority for your life is that you become fruitful. For that result, four seasons are required. Four physical seasons produce one harvest. If you miss any of the four seasons, you don't receive a harvest. If no winter exists, a harvest doesn't exist either. Winter replenishes and renews the earth, transforming what had been growing—trees, bushes, grass—into rich, fertile soil. Spring is a time of planting, so there can be growth in the summer and harvest in the fall. Spring is the season of hope, patience, and waiting. You need to get through every season, even if you don't see anything occurring, or anything good happening. Embrace your season and trust God.

Every season of life has fruit.

Every season of life will have provision and challenges, as well as potential. Some seasons are forced upon you and you have no choice. You don't have any control; however, you can determine your response, even if a season is forced upon you. It is also possible for you to forcefully create a new season in your life.

You will create a new season in your life only when the season that you are in becomes too painful for you to stay there. God's purpose for challenges is to create a change in how a person is living his or her life. God is always calling you to leave the average, mundane, mediocre life, which the vast majority of human beings on the planet live. You can change the unfruitful seasons of pain, disappointment, confusion, conflict, and lack. Create a new season of adventure—experience extraordinary achievements.

God's idea of your new season may not be just what you're wanting, but He desires what He desires for you. He doesn't just arbitrarily give you your request. God says, "You just want to escape, but I want to put you on display and show the world what I do with my Diamond Life people." You build your legacy as you live.

Waiting is a season of life. Life is made of time. Time is valuable and important for every significant achievement in your life. Without millions of years of time, no diamond would even exist.

The quality of your life depends upon the investment of your time. For example, at the end of a day you could say to yourself, "What did I exchange this day for, and was it worth it?" The difference between people is not in their opportunities, but it is in the ability to recognize and take hold of an opportunity. Every season of life is filled with opportunity and potential; every season is a learning experience.

Reflecting on the night he was chosen to be prime minister of Britain, in the dark days marking England's full-fledged entry into World War II, Winston Churchill wrote, "I felt as if I were walking with destiny and that all my past life had been but a preparation for this hour and this trial."

God gets you ready for your seasons. Every previous season of your life has actually prepared you for your "now season." All of your life, up until now, is crammed into your current moment.

- Am I conforming when I could be transforming?
- Am I advancing or retreating?
- Am I passive or active?

I see my way as birds their trackless way.
I shall arrive,—what time, what circuit first,
I ask not; but unless God send his hail
Or blinding fire-balls, sleet or stifling snow,
In some good time, his good time, I shall arrive:
He guides me and the bird. In his good time.

—ROBERT BROWNING

Robert Browning wrote in *Paracelsus*, these lines:

In essence, he is saying, "Nothing is going to stop me on my journey. I am going to move into my moment. I am going to move into my strategic position. I am going to get there." There is a constant danger of making my current season (my circumstance, moment) my destiny.

The seasons of life reveal your identity, your purpose, and your destiny. Hundreds of years ago, Isaiah gave a formula for living through the seasons of life.

> *But those who wait for the Lord [who expect, look for, and hope in Him], they shall change and renew their strength and their power; They shall lift their wings and mount up [close to God] as eagles [mount up to the sun]; they shall run and not be weary, they shall walk and they shall not faint or become tired (Isaiah 40:31, AMP).*

His message was concerning change and renewal in order to regain strength and position.

Isaiah put this sequence of movement into a descending order: flying, running, walking. Perhaps some would have inverted the order to read:

- ♦ They shall walk and not faint.
- ♦ They shall run and not be weary.
- ♦ They shall mount up with wings as eagles.

♦ They shall fly up towards the sun.

That seems more logical, a more reasonable process. However, God is not always logical or reasonable. He defies logic and reason. As humans, we often begin a great endeavor with expectations and enthusiasm that are high and lofty-stratospheric. The sky is the limit. We are consumed with glorious ambitions. We are full of confidence that we are going to achieve them no matter what. We are soaring and *flying* high with the big picture, the big possibility. However, in order to execute the plan, we discover we must slow the pace, narrow the focus.

In the process of pursuing the high-flying ambition, we begin to run with it. While this is quite different from the high enthusiasm and excitement level of *flying*, it is a necessary step toward further rational, reasonable thinking and planning. This is a more controlled phase. It is enthusiastic, but more detailed.

The next step is *walking*, which means we have come through the high emotional start of a grand idea to the energy of running with it and pursuing it. Now we enter the sometimes tedious stage of walking out the plan. This is the most important part of any grand idea. That's why life is sometimes referred to as a walk, such as the walk of life. Any grand ambition that doesn't get walked out step by step will not bring a positive result. Thus it is, with all of grand ambitions—fly, run, walk.

Look carefully then how you walk! Live purposefully and worthily and accurately, not as the unwise and witless, but as wise (sensible, intelligent people), Making the very most of the time [buying up each opportunity], because the days are evil (Ephesians 5:15, 16, AMP).

The Latin expression of that sentiment is *Carpe Diem*—"seize the day." The only way you can "seize the day" is to be "present in the present." You have to be "alive in the moment." You have to be "aware of what's going on."

There are no "unspecial" moments in life.

Your life is filled with unlimited possibility, which must be integrated with human accountability. The Divine Creator invested gifts, talents, and abilities into your life that can make the world a better place.

The most important principle for human growth and development that you will ever learn is your response to your seasons. No one, no circumstance, no challenge should ever diminish your value as a person. God, who made you, assigns human value and nothing in your life should ever reduce that value. Remember, nothing ever gets into your life without coming through His hand. That which comes through His hand into your life is never meant to decrease you, only to increase you—make you more, make you better. Your season has a purpose.

Your season has a reason. Be present in the present and embrace your season. Occupy, recognize, and understand why and where you are. The season of sowing is the season of promise. The seeds you are sowing today produce your future. If you know where you are going and where you have been, you never have to fear where you are.

All of life is a process. The progression of the seasons reveals the divine plan of the Creator—everything is about process. You can never look at your life in an isolated moment and say, "This is my life." Say instead, "This is only a season in my life. I am going through a process." Never judge your life by one season. Wait until you go through at least four seasons. Wait until some kind of crop is produced through your life so you can see the harvest of that season; for every season can have a harvest.

You determine the value of you;
you determine the value of your time;
you determine the quality of your effort.

The Greeks had a unique way of thinking about time. They used two words—"*chronos*" and "*kairos*." "*Chronos*" time is a series of events in life, the chronology of life. The chronology of life is the minutes, hours, days, weeks, months, years. "*Kairos*" refers to quality moment times, a high-energy moment, an impact moment. Perhaps I could call it an epiphany—a marked, distinct moment in time.

In the process of your lifetime, there will be moments when you experience lack. Lack should never be seen as a destination, but a temporary moment. In the process of developing The Diamond Life, there will be times when you must be totally dependent on the unseen working of God. You and I come possessed with a download of eternal software. God should become more real than the physical things around us. In His Kingdom (where you should be living), there is never a lack, never a recession, never a depression. There is always provision.

When God is your reality, you will see the invisible–His provision produced in your life by the sowing of seed. You will see the need, but look beyond the need to God. Your harvest is always dependent on your sowing. Your seed is your gifts, talents and abilities, which are mere possibilities until sown into the soil of opposition.

The Beauty of Dirt

The value of winter was vividly shown to me on a trip to Israel. One day while we were traveling, our Jewish guide, Gideon, responded to my question concerning all the rocks that were rising up from the ground by asking me, "Don't you know where dirt comes from?" "Of course," I replied, "I know where dirt comes from." But then, I wondered: where does dirt actually come from?

When the Turkish Empire conquered Israel, they cut

down the trees. Without the growth of trees, there is no production of dirt. The trees grow and produce fruit, leaves, limbs, and then die and decompose. Thus, they create rich dirt. Since there were few trees, very little dirt existed and eventually the land of Israel became mostly rocks. No civilization can survive without dirt. While no one would ever call dirt beautiful, it is the essence of life. Perhaps it should not be called dirt, but beautiful, rich soil. There is no better commodity than rich, black soil. How valuable the winter season becomes! Though you may look around and discover little progress, little production, no visible harvest, yet, that season has value. Winter permits the earth to rest, to replenish itself.

Winter is a season in which many people get discouraged because of a lack of harvest. Winter creates fertile, enriched, black soil. During winter, the food systems of the trees become dormant and dead leaves and branches fall onto the ground and decompose to create more valuable, enriched soil. Therefore, in essence, the diamond passes through several seasons. Each of those seasons adds value to the diamond. Its hardness, brilliance, weight, and value are determined through the millions of years of heat, pressure, and time.

At any given phase, the diamond is not a completed work. There may be moments of lack between the piece of coal and the processed diamond, but the journey doesn't end until it becomes a finished product. It is through the process of discovery, that the diamond can be seen in its most valuable state. God's most challenging task for you and I is to unearth the treasure within us so that we can be strategically placed and seen by the world.

Sow His truth into your life today and be transformed as His seed produces a miracle for your need.

A seed goes through a similar process. A seed does not look like the soil, much like a piece of coal does not look like a diamond. The soil does not look like the seed. There is nothing about a seed that remotely reflects the soil. They are two extremely different substances. However, when the seed is dropped into the soil, rain comes down from the heaven, and the warmth of the sun heats up the soil. At this moment, germination occurs and a sprout comes out of the ground. What's amazing about this is that the soil was made for the seed and the seed was made for the soil.

Each of them has its own unique qualities that cannot be released until they come together under the proper conditions (the right season). Until the seed is in the ground at the proper season, at the right time, under the right conditions with water and sun, neither of them can release their potential. But the moment they come together, suddenly the inactive seed comes to life and interacts with the soil.

Daily you are sowing the seed of your life into the soil of circumstance, challenge, victory, trial, joy, adversity, peace, triumph. Once you sow "you," what happens to you is the same thing that happens to the seed. You release your potential (your soil) and produce The Diamond Life you were created for.

**You never just sow what you have;
you sow who you are.**

The fruit of your life is the result of the seed of your daily choices and behaviors. Inside of each person is a seed that can become the answer to his or her need. The reason you have a need in your life is because God desires to release a seed already in your possession. Think about that!

See yourself as a seed. Look at your life and see the needs of your life. God has permitted a need in your life because within your possession is a seed He wants released. As you sow your gifts, your talents, your abilities—you—into the soil of life, you receive the provision of your need. The proof of your sowing is a harvest. If you sow, you grow, and so do those around you. It is the process of life.

Your need is an attempt by God to reveal the hidden resources which can only be discovered when you sow the seed of your life. When you sow your life, you reap something so beautiful, so glorious, and far beyond the ugly dirt and the shriveled-up, dried seed. There is no comparison of the beauty of the two with the beauty of the harvest that is produced. You are unique. Your seed is unique. It is not going to be like anyone else's. God's harvest for you is unique, special, beyond comparison.

Our destiny is produced by the seeds we are sowing today.

I remember a *kairos* moment when God caused me to understand my life as a seed. Suddenly, I knew that He could sow my life into any soil (challenge, circumstance, difficulty, adversity) and cause me to produce a harvest as I put my trust in Him. My only purpose in being here is for the Sower of Heaven to sow the seed of my life, in order to reap His purpose.

The Victory is Yours

The truth is you are powerful, influential with potential beyond your wildest imagination. Your life is filled with value, worth. Maybe as you look at your current condition, you don't see it, but neither would you see in a black lump of coal the value of a sparkling diamond.

Your life is either going to be filled with great abundance or great lack depending on your response to His purpose in your life. He said your life will either be filled with great abundance or great lack depending upon your response to God's truth. In 1 Corinthians 3:9 (AMP), "He declares that you are God's garden and vineyard and field under cultivation."

What is He saying? You are not perfected. He said, "I

am growing a harvest with your life. I am producing something with your life. I am allowing your life to be sown into all kinds of situations in order to produce a harvest for my glory."

A field under cultivation doesn't always look like a desired harvest.

What do you desire?

Do you have a desire to live a Diamond Life?

Would you like your life to be maximized to the fullest potential?

Would you like your life to matter and make a difference?

Then you should realize each person is born with greater potential than he or she has ever experienced. Sometimes it is necessary to do a self-inventory; an introspection of your life to determine the extent of your current reality.

- ♦ Where am I in relationship to my circumstances?
- ♦ Where am I in relationship to where I could be?
- ♦ Where am I in relationship to my value?
- ♦ Why am I here?
- ♦ Why was I born?

- ♦ What is my purpose?
- ♦ What is my potential?

The answer to each one of those questions, you must take full advantage of every season in your life. You are born with greater potential than you will ever experience. There is more to you than you will ever know. Most people die without ever having reached their fullest potential. Somewhere along the way, they settled and gave up, quit, or whatever; they just didn't get there.

Every day you are sowing your life by the thoughts you think, by the words you speak, and the actions you take. Regardless of your season, you are one word from God away from total victory—just one seed from God away from your harvest. Your very next season could be one of harvest-that is the only reason for your season.

Ann Marie, Dylan and Leah, along with Sean and Lisa lived this very process. Though each of them faced great challenges, which ultimately could have destroyed their lives, they lived through the winter season and discovered the beauty of the promise of spring. And today, they are reaping the harvest of their Diamond Life.

This could very well be your story, starting today. The very reason for this book is the truth that God intended for all of us to live The Diamond Life. You can never expect to advance, unless you start.

LIFE GEMS

From Chapter Twelve

Always embrace your seasons.

Recognize your P.E.T.

Seasons develop and mature you.

Waiting is a season of life.

Seasons reveal your identity,
purpose, and destiny.

Your season has a reason.

See yourself as a seed.

LIVE THE DIAMOND LIFE

The worth, the value of your life causes you to be a light in a dark world.

Just as the world was in darkness, and God spoke His light, you, too, must become light so the world can see the true value of The Diamond Life. Just imagine a million, 10 million, a billion Diamond Life people suddenly becoming *The Light Fix* the world so desperately needs. Perhaps that could even be the next chapter in your life.

GLOSSARY OF IMPORTANT WORDS

The Diamond Life Formula

The process by which a lump of coal is subjected to heat, pressure and time until it becomes a valuable diamond. The same applies to each life.

Direction

Guidance gained from the Bible and the Holy Spirit.

GPS (Global Positioning System)

A satellite-based navigation system that enables users to identify a specific location on earth.

Identity

As used in this book, the awareness of a person of who he or she is in Christ.

LSQ (Life Satisfaction Quotient)

The extent to which a person feels a sense of fulfillment in his or her present state of existence.

M.A.P (Master-Assigned Path)

The paths God has chosen you to walk in.

PBS (Personal Belief System)

Those things which you have come to believe concerning any subject.

P.D.T. (Personal Discipleship Time)

Whatever the season, God helps you maneuver through it.

P.E.T. (Personal Empowerment Time)

It is in the moment when you don't like a season that it is most likely going to empower you.

Protection

Divine security by God against any threat or difficulty.

Provision

Divine supply by God for any area of human need.

Purpose

As used in this book, the reason a person is created by God.

Spirit Life-Coach

The ministry of the Holy Spirit of helping Christ-followers know how to live.

IF YOU LIKED THIS BOOK

- Go to my facebook page, **facebook.com/pastortonyscott** and click like and post a comment regarding what you enjoyed about the book.
- Tweet quotes using **@pastortonyscott** and comments using hashtag **#DiamondLifeBook**
- Interested in additional copies of *The Diamond Life Book, You are more than you have become*, go to **www.thediamondlifebook.com**
- Download the eBook at **www.thediamondlifebook.com**
- Contact thediamondlifebook@gmail.com

www.TheDiamondLifeBook.com

iBank

Planet earth was designed with enormous wealth and treasure for the purpose of enriching the life of man. This is the wealthiest planet in the universe and it was made for us. God never intended for anyone to be in poverty. Are you ready to become "Fiscally Fit?" This series of messages from Tony Scott will reveal the path to financial freedom. **6 CD's $25**

No Limits

How high do you want to climb? How far do you want to go? How much do you want to achieve? What are your limits? Come on a journey toward the "No Limits" Life. By changing your thinking you change your results and thus change your life. **7 CD's $30**

Take Action

Are you getting out of life what you want? Are you experiencing satisfaction? In Latin "statis" means "enough." The last six letters spell "action." Enough action ultimately produces "satisfaction." Every achievement in life is the result of some action. Take Action and achieve your dreams.
4 CD's $20

The Increase Life Book

The whole message of the Bible about increase is a message about whole-life increase – every area of your life, all of your life. The Bible message about increase has to do with who you are and who you become. It has to do with what you do with the natural talents and spiritual gifts that God gives to you. It has to do with the influence you have, the leadership you exert, and the things you accomplish for God's Kingdom. **$10**

ABOUT THE AUTHOR

Tony Scott is recognized nationally and internationally as a teacher, mentor, visionary leader and successful author. His message centers on the balanced life – Spirit, Soul & Body.

His travels have taken him to some ten nations on five continents. Hundreds of thousands of people have been impacted by these practical principles for living a life of significance.

Scott resides with his wife, ShirleyAnn in Toledo, Ohio. Together they provide spiritual leadership to hundreds of families through multi-site campuses.